Table of Contents

Introduction

I write this on behalf of the many believers that are in law enforcement all over the world. They have picked up their crosses and dare to follow Christ. It is Jesus Christ who has chosen us and we accepted. We endeavor to be the good men and women that the Bible speaks about when David said, *"the steps of a good man are ordered by the Lord: and he delighteth in his way. Though he falls, he shall not be utterly cast down: for the Lord upholdeth him with his hand"* (**Psalms 37:23-24, KJV**).

It is Christ who leads us and it is Christ in whom we follow. He is our Leader, Guide, Counselor, Savior, Friend and the Head of our lives. We put our trust in the Lord and believe that, *"he will never leave us nor forsake us."* I know that with God all things are possible, but without him we can do nothing.

Though the job of a Law Enforcement Officer can be dangerous and challenging, again I turn to God's word for courage: *"The Lord is my light and my salvation; whom shall I fear? The Lord is the strength of my life of whom shall I be afraid? When the wicked came against me to eat up my flesh, my enemies and foes, they stumbled and fell. Though an army should encamp against me, my heart shall not fear; though war should rise against me, in this I will be confident. One thing I have desired of the Lord, that will I seek: That I may dwell in the house of the Lord All the days of my life..."* (**Psalms 27:1-4, NKJV**).

WARNING: Please note that some of the dialogue during the interviews may contain actual words used in that conversation and may be offensive to some. I have tried to cleanup the language as much as possible without reducing or enhancing the person's true character. It is important however that some of the dialogue be left unchanged for the reader to correctly perceive the character of the person engaged.

The names were changed or nicknames are used to protect the innocent and the guilty; so by any chance the attitude or character of any of these individuals is similar to yours, remember there are people that act just like you all over the world. We must understand that if it wasn't for the Lord many of us would read about these different cases and say, **"but for the grace and mercy of God, that could be me."**

Chapter I
The birth of an Officer

I was born in Crockett Texas and I am told it was named after Davy Crockett. At the age of six months old my parents came to Arizona by way of New Mexico. Our family was very poor and being Black made things even worse. I was the youngest of eleven children.

I don't know much about the journey or the reason we left Texas, but somewhere along the way we landed in Continental, Arizona. We lived on the other side of the tracks with other Black, Hispanic and Native American families. My dad was a farm hand and my mother normally worked in the fields. I can actually remember positioning myself on the end of her cotton sack and sleeping as she picked cotton and pulled me along. Sometimes my older sister would care for us at the car while they worked. They would park the car at the end of the cotton rows and come and see about us when ever they weighed their cotton sacks or when they had chopped to the end of their row. It depended on rather they were picking cotton or chopping it.

My mom had two sets of children. She had married my father after being a widow. My brothers and sisters by her first marriage had children my age. The children by my father had totaled four: two boys and two girls.

I learned many lessons while in the small community of Continental and one of them was if you live, death is imminent. **I learned that if you die in Christ, this earth is the only hell you have to worry about, but if you die out of the will of God then this is your only heaven.**

My mother was a Christian and her faith in God was immeasurable. Most of our teaching and Christian up bringing came from her, but my father did contribute quite a bit to our morals, values and ethics. We learned from dad what not to do.

I have learned that if you live long enough adversity is inevitable, and anyone God takes from this earth can never truly be replaced. The void they leave can be filled, but no one can be replaced. The greatest irreversible tragedy is the lost of a loved one or a family member. Such a lost occurred prior to my illness, which came from an outbreak of typhoid.

My sister Bernie (Bernice) was called by the Death Angel. I believe that everyone, prior to death, hear the call of the Death Angel or the Angel of Death. Few people listen and know that the end is near and others know, but they refuse to listen. I guess the idea of death knocking on your door isn't very encouraging.

The things people do prior to their death are amazing. When the Death Angel calls, people do the strangest things in preparation after that calling. Some people clean up their homes or do clean up details in their lives. Some have financial layouts prepared. They give away things that you never thought they would part with. The most precious and cherished possessions are passed on to others simply because the Death Angel knocked on life's door and they heard.

It is very mysterious, the reactions of individuals who know they are going to die. As an officer I went to many D.O.A calls (Dead on Arrival) and noticed that many people had made plans before death made its arrival. There were those times when death came unannounced and there wasn't time to prepare, or did they just forget to listen the first time death knocked?

The following is exerts from my book, "Toeboys Growing up," by Lacey Colter Sr. (Codas):

Bernie was my seventeen year old sister. She was a very beautiful girl just beginning her life and full of hope. She was just married and had a six-month-old son.

One day the Death Angel spoke to Bernie and from that moment her behavior became very strange. She would answer aloud, "Yes, what do you want...who called?" She would question us to see if we had called her name.

I am reminded of the story in the Bible (1Sam: 3:4). Samuel was just a child when he first heard God speaking to him. Samuel would awaken from his sleep and go to Eli the priest and say, "here am I." Eli would tell Samuel "go back and lie down." He had no idea what Samuel was talking about. After the third time Eli perceived that the Lord had called the child and told him to respond by saying, *"speak Lord; for thy servant heareth."* Samuel did so and God spoke to him. This is what Bernie was going through. The voice she heard was that of the Death Angel.

Later that day Bernie was at home with her six month old son, my sister Mary and me. We were eight and three years old respectively. I can vividly recall the events of that tragic day. A loud voice shouted out her name and as we turned, standing in the doorway was her husband Frank. He was intoxicated and possessed with evil intent. He was in a rage, swearing and grabbing and throwing things. He banished a weapon (handgun) from nowhere and pointed it at her and threatened to kill her.

"I could kill you if I wanted to," he cried out!

She reminded him, "there are children in the room honey and you need to put the gun away."

"You don't think I will shoot you bitch," he blurted through his slurred speech?

"I'm asking you to put the gun away before someone gets hurt," she responded in a calm but nervous voice.

I have never known why he was in such a rage, but I heard Bernie pleading with him to put the gun down. He cursed and planted himself in the doorway to block our exit. He then fired twice and Bernie felt the impact of both bullets as they tore into her upper body. One bullet grazed the navel of the child she was holding in her arms and continued to penetrate Bernie's upper body.

4

The baby started screaming with pain due to the heat of the bullet severing part of his navel. The blood squirted from his wound. Bernie was knocked backwards by the impact of the shots and was covered with blood. She held on to the baby and laid him on the Bed and staggered to the doorway. The blood began to saturate her clothing as it gushed forth like a dam releasing its waters. She brushed by Frank who was standing there holding the gun as if it was a stranger to him. He stared at the weapon then he looked at Bernie as if he was thinking, *"I wished I hadn't done that!"* She walked passed him never looking at him at all, but having her eyes and mind fixed on her destination. I followed her as she slowly stumbled to the barracks next door to where Mom and Dad were. They were concern about the noise they had just heard, but the last thing on their mind was the thought that their child had been shot.

"Mama, Mama," cried Bernie, while leaning against the raggedy screen door that had seen its last days. With all her strength she had made it next door to the attached barrack where we lived. With all her life oozing out of her body she fell against the screen door and using every ounce of her strength she was barely able to turn the knob and open the door. Slowly she staggered inside. Everything she touched was scarlet red with her blood, which profusely poured from her body like a fountain. The blood was leaving stains on everything she touched. Her clothes were soaking up the blood but the clothes could soak no more as the essence of life flowed from her open wounds. She lifted her feet slowly to take the next step and her footprint would quickly fill with blood. This was an indication that the bullets had pierced through her heart. The steps that Bernie took to get to Mama's arms were outlined in red. The imprint of her every step contained drops of Bernie's life being left behind on the ground.

My father sitting in a chair was petrified and speechless while watching Bernie as she entered the room. She leaned backwards against the wall with no more strength she slid down the wall to her knees and fell forward across my father's lap. Daddy sat in total disbelief as he touched Bernie and then examined the color of his hands. His hands were covered with the blood of his daughter. She was crying softly, but in a soft and weak voice she spoke to Mama who was across the room.

"Mama I've been shot! Mama I've been shot," was the whisper that came from the lips of her dying child.

Mama ran from across the room to where Bernie was lying crouched over Daddy's lap. Dad sat there horrified and in shock. The tears begin flowing from his eyes like rivers of water as he began to perceive the reality of the situation. Mama ran to Bernie lifting her up into her arms and they both fell against the wall. They were pressed against the wall and both slid down the wall with Bernie still in Mama's arms. Bernie's blood was smeared against the wall and it appeared much darker than before.

"No God, not my baby, please God not my baby, my baby!" cried Mama.

Bernie lay there in Mama's arms; these loving and gentle arms that had held her for many years as a child and now unto death.

Just a few days earlier she had rested in those same arms as she told Mama about the voice of the Death Angel. Yes, even unto death Mama's arms comforted Bernice. They both sat on the floor in each other's arms covered in the scarlet essence of life that drained from Bernie. The tears flowed softly and both hearts beat together. Soon only one heart would continue to beat. For one last time, Bernice looked into the tear stained face of a grieving mother about to lose a piece of her heart.

"Mama, I've been shot. It's gonna be all right Mama, it's gonna be all right," she whispered softly. Now, it was Bernie who was trying to comfort Mama.

Then I heard Mama plead to God one last time for the life of her child.

"No God, please, not my baby my baby!"

Bernie continued to gaze into the face of grief and eyes that were flooded with tears. She said, "Mama it's okay, I'm going home," and she slowly closed her eyes.

Both of their hearts beat frantically and then one slowed until there was only one heart beating. Bernie eyes were now closed forever and her heart ceased to beat and she released into the air her last breath.

I believe for a brief moment Mama's heart stopped too. She died with Bernie for a little while. Bernie's body grew limp and she appeared relaxed for the first time since she heard the call of the Death Angel. She now heard the voice of the heavenly choir singing softly as she made her entrance unto the presence of God. Her spirit was now free. That day Bernie's *spirit returned to God whom gave it* (Ecclesiastes 12:7, KJV; "Toeboys Growing up" permitted by author Lacey Colter Sr. "Codas").

My sister Mary testified against Frank and he was convicted of first-degree murder and was sentenced to life in prison. His only defense was, **"It was an accident; I was drunk."** One thing I do know is you don't shoot someone multiple times on accident, unless it's an automatic weapon and by some phenomenon your finger gets stuck on the trigger.

This was my first look at a crime and at the results of law and order. I thought one day, maybe, I would be a person who would solve crimes and save lives. It was apparent that one Black person killing another did not receive very much attention in those days. I guess some people would say that is even true today in some places. I do know that the incident did create a dissonance between family members. It also remained a mystery to many, as to why it happened. It was a big shock that he got twenty years to life for the murder of his wife, because black on black crime wasn't taken very serious in the late 1940s and early 1950s.

Twenty years later after coming home from college, while on break, I saw a strange man in our house. My sister Lillie was there and was furious and it seemed that one word would have created an explosion from her.

It was common for my mother to feed strangers and send them on their way. It seemed that every stray animal knew our address as well.

I waited for a moment then asked, "Who is the guy at the table eating and why is mom giving him clothes?"

"It's the S.O.B. that killed our sister," she blurted out loud! It seemed that she wanted him to hear.

"It's who!" I shouted, as the memories begin to flood my mind and my heart was overwhelmed with resentment? How could my mother allow the man that killed her daughter to come into our home? How could she forgive such a person as this and show him charity and mercy?

I watched as he filled his belly with our food and my mother gave him a few dollars, some clothes and sent him on his way, just as she would do to any other homeless person in need.

"What's he doing here," I asked?

"He just got out of prison and the first place he came was here," shouted my sister. "You know mama; she'll help anything; a stray dog or cat and even a murderer."

I waited for a while and then went inside. I was about to ask mama about the man, but she interrupted me.

"For if you forgive men their trespasses, your heavenly Father will also forgive you, but if you do not forgive men their trespasses, neither will your Father forgive your trespasses" (Matthew 6:14-15, KJV), she said, "That's from the Bible you know?"

"Yes," I belted, "but that was concerning people not animals and he is a…."

Again she interrupted me, *"be ye therefore merciful as your father also is merciful. Judge not, and you shall not be judged. Condemn not, and you shall not be condemned. Forgive, and you will be forgiven. Give, and it will be given to you: good measure, pressed down, shaken together and running over...for with the same measure that you use, it will be measured back to you"* (Luke 6:36-38, KJV).

After hearing those words I knew my mother was doing what she thought was right in her heart, so I walked away. I don't think it was me, but the Spirit of God that turned me around and led me out of the room.

It was then that I understood what the Apostle Paul was talking about when he said, *"Though I speak with the tongues of men and of angels, but have not love, I have become as sounding brass or a clanging cymbal. And though I have the gift of prophecy, and understand all mysteries and all knowledge, and though I have all faith, so that I could remove mountains, but have not love, I am nothing. And though I bestow all my goods to feed the poor, and though I give my body to be burned, but have not love, it profits me nothing. Love suffers long and is kind; love does not envy; love does not parade itself, is not puffed up; does not behave rudely, does not seek its own, is not provoked, thinks no evil; does not rejoice in iniquity, but rejoices in the truth; bears all things, believes all things, hopes all things, endures all things. Love never fails"* **(NKJV, 1Corinthians 13:1-8).**

I never saw this man again, but I did see the many stray animals, and the other transients and hobos that my mother fed and clothed throughout her life. She had a heart of gold and only God can place a value on the heart of a person. I am told that Frank had gotten involved in a relationship with another woman and the irony is, after having a conflict, and when she got fed up with him she shot him in the face with a shotgun. That day when he departed from the world, he had to stand before the greatest judge of all, Jesus Christ.

I pray that perhaps during his stay in prison he asked God for forgiveness, and he had the opportunity to accept Christ as his Savior. If he did, he still had a problem, "shacking up." I am reminded of Judas Iscariot, who betrayed Christ; he repented and then went and hung himself (he committed self murder).

Chapter II
Called by God

At the age of five years old I became ill with typhoid fever. I was hospitalized for several months. I became so sick that I was given two weeks to live. My parents decided to take me home at the advice of the doctors and let me spend my last days at home with the family.

I was crippled, deaf in one ear and partially blind as a result of the illness. I sensed a degree of prejudice/discrimination when I left the hospital, because the White kids who were unable to walk were given a wheel chair or crutches. I had to rely on a stick I found on the ground to hold me up. I also remember how cruel children can be, because they would jump over me as I lie on the ground and would laugh and called me names.

I'm glad I had a praying mother who was determined to take my case before God. She believed that God would spare my life because he wanted to do a work in me.

We went to every revival that came to town. One night she took me to a tent revival and the preacher prayed for me. He prophesied and said God had a calling on my life. He asked God to spare my life, because I was so young and take his instead. Can you imagine that?

You better be careful how you pray and what you say, because you may get what you asked for. Mother told me later that she heard that the preacher had died suddenly. It seemed that it was on that day that I started getting better. I can truly say that I made it past the two weeks and with my deaf ear I heard his calling, with my blind eye I saw the light and those lame legs now carry the gospel of Jesus Christ.

God has always provided for me since I was a child. Since God had delivered me from the clutches of death as a child, I have always had a hotline to heaven. At the age of twelve I talked to the Lord daily as I would a friend. It seemed that whatsoever I asked for concerning the necessities of life God provided.

My parents were poor, but most of the time we had something to eat. Many times it wasn't what I wanted, but it was food. On several occasions I would go home after playing most of the day and there was no food cooked. Mom and dad were working in the fields and we had to wait until they came home. There were always potatoes and a few eggs from the few chickens we raised. Most of the time there was water to make Kool-aide. Sometimes when I got home from a hard day of playing with my friends there was nothing. I would check the chicken coup to see if there were any eggs or the garden to see if anything was there to eat. I would either have to wait until my mother got home or ask God for help, and most of the time I would ask God for help.

My sister Lillie and I had a sibling rivalry going on and since she was older than me, she thought she had the upper hand. She would cook up everything and eat it just for spite. I would ask God for food, and He would always provide for me. One day after coming home to nothing to eat, I told Lillie that I had prayed and God said I would find the money on the way to the store. She would always mock me and say, "you done lost your mind!" When I came back from the store with bologna ends and a box of crackers it would shut her up for a moment. Later she would accuse me of stealing the food or stealing the money to buy it. I believe if I would have ever went to court for something **I didn't do,** my sister Lillie would have testified against me.

The truth was that the Lord would speak to me and tell me *"go to the store and you will find the money on the way."* Now let's be honest, I didn't hear a voice from heaven, but there was that voice that speaks from within. Every time I went I would find the money along the way as I walked through the desert trail. Now this wasn't something I did everyday, but once in a while, and I did it in faith.

When I would return home with food, Lou (Lillie's middle name) would begin accusing me of being a thief. I would always respond in a way that really ticked her off.

I would look up to the sky and point with one finger, indicating that my blessing came from above.

"Ask and it shall be given unto you," I said. "Seek and ye shall find, knock and the door shall be open unto you."

She would respond, "Yeah right! You didn't ask you just took it. You did seek and you found it in the store; you don't have to knock if you're already inside and it wasn't given to you, you stole it."

I retorted sarcastically, **"O ye of little faith, nappy hair, bad breath and an ugly face, I beseech thee to shut up, if thou carest to partake of my offerings."** I felt if I spoke in King James rhetoric it would be more affective, and she would think I was quoting a scripture.

On one occasion I was very hungry and when I got home mom and dad were at work and Lou had eaten everything. I think sometimes she did it just to see if God would answer my prayers. This time I prayed and the Lord said, *"Go and wait and I will provide for you."* I made the mistake of telling Lou what God said to me.

Lou began teasing and said, "Just as sure as you are Black when you leave here, you'll be Blacker when you return. Fool, you're going there hungry and you're coming back hungry. God don't talk to the poor, stupid, and ignorant little black children like yourself; He talks to the rich white kids or Jews like Moses and Elijah."

"You just wait," I said, "I might be Black when I leave and Black when I return, and I might leave here hungry, but I won't come back the same way. We'll see who is poor, stupid and ignorant when I return with food, O great wicked witch of the Toe" (short for the town of Rilli**to**).

She would then throw me the finger and having her index finger pointing at me, she would say, "Take this with you!"

I went along the way expecting to find money as always or run into one of the guys who had a nickel or dime to spare. I walked the entire distance and found nothing. I looked inside the store to see if one of my buddies were there and saw no one. All I could hear was Lou's voice, "you're going there Black and you're coming back Blacker; fool, you're going there hungry and you're coming back hungry, and God don't talk to the poor, stupid and ignorant..."

I heard a quiet and still voice speak to my heart after Lou's voice stopped yelling in my ear. The voice said, *"I told you to go and wait and I will provide for you!"*

It's amazing that when Satan speaks to us he yells, but when God speaks it's always a quiet and still voice.

While I waited at the store, I notice a White man who was dressed moderately but was driving a new car. He had the appearance of someone who was wealthy. He was inside the telephone booth making some calls. He seemed very disappointed and banged against the telephone as he spoke. When he exited the booth he made a futile attempt to slam the folding doors.

I continued waiting as I was instructed until it began to rain. I didn't have any place to go for shelter. The store clerk was suspicious and I was too embarrassed to go inside without any money. My only other alternative was the telephone booth.

I found shelter in the booth, and I starred out at the monsoon storm that instantly came up. While in the booth I turned towards the phone and there was change on the shelf. I was excited and as I turned to open the folded door I bumped the telephone box. I heard a jingling sound like money falling through the phone, but I couldn't see anything. I stuck my finger in the change return and there was more change. It totaled fifty cents, which was more than enough for me to get some food in the 1950's. My parents worked in the fields for less than five dollars a day, so fifty cents was a lot of money for a child.

I returned home hoping that the storm had taken the house away with Lou in it, but unfortunately it didn't. I did buy enough for both of us and shared it with her when I got home. I had read in the bible: *"if thine enemy hunger, feed him; if he thirst, give him drink: for in so doing thou shalt heap coals of fire on his head"* **(Romans 12:20, KJV)**. There was nothing that I would enjoy more than heaping coals of fire on Lou's head.

There were times when I would be playing with the guys and Lou would call me home. She pretended as if it was something important just to get me home. When I got there she would say sarcastically, "Why don't you ask the Lord for some money so I can go buy some candy?"

"It doesn't work like that," I said.

"How does it work," she demanded?

"God gives me what I need," I replied, "and candy ain't on the list."

"Get it on the stinking list, you bum!" she shouted.

"Get your own list!" I shouted back at her, disappointed that she had interrupted my playing time.

"I'll make up my own stinking list, you little brat!" she snarled, "and I will tell God that you wrote it."

"God knows when the devil is in his presence, so don't bother with the list," I belted as I slammed the door and returned to playing with my friends.

There were many blessings bestowed on me as a child as I grew up in the Community of Rillito, Arizona. Many of us became athletes and made a name for ourselves in High School and in the Pros. The boys of the "Toe" had a bond that could never be broken. We loved each other and still do. There are many stories of the trials and tribulations of our youth, but God always delivered us. We never knew we were poor until we left home and went beyond the boundaries of the community.

My father died when I was a freshman in High School and we lived off social security and the money we received from working in the cotton fields. My sister Mary helped out until she got married and had a family of her own. My brother Butch was a taker and not a giver. He was his own little world, but every now and then he showed a glimpse of compassion. In fact, he bought me a suit when I graduated from High School, and I didn't have to pay him back.

I played sports and was able to get an athletic scholarship to attend Northern Arizona University. Thanks be to God! I also got married to my childhood sweetheart. My sister Lou, who was now my greatest fan, allowed us to stay a week in her apartment as a wedding present. Though she was still mischievous, she had my mother's heart.

While attending Northern Arizona University the athletes would work summer employment at the mines in the areas of Southern Arizona. After graduating from the University and a brief stay with a Professional Football Team I was offered a job at American Smelter and Refining Company (ASARCO). In those days I signed as a free agent for twelve thousand dollars a year, but when I went to work for the mines my salary was fifteen thousand dollars. Amazing, I made more money working at the mines than playing professional football.

I accepted Christ in my life and several times I went on a twenty-one day fast. After fasting for twenty-one days I decided to try and start eating the right things. I went for over a year eating fish and salads and taking vitamin after vitamin to ensure a good and healthy body. What I didn't realize was I had overdosed on fish and vitamins and everything reached the point of diminishing returns *(Diminishing Return is that point when the benefit you receive from what you're doing begins to diminish to the point of detriment. Example: one scoop of ice-cream could be nourishing for the body, but somewhere between one scoop and two gallons you reach a point of diminishing return).*

I broke out with hives all over my body and labored with my breathing. The itching was so terrible that I found myself jogging down the road and tears flowing due to the discomfort. When I got home afterwards it was difficult to distinguish the tears on my face from the sweat.

I went from doctor to doctor trying to find out what caused this allergic reaction within my body. Finally I was tested and found I was highly allergic to fish. Well, I had been eating fish for years and taking fish oil pills along with different vitamins. The Doctor informed me that I could overdose on vitamins like a person overdose on drugs. He also advised me that I was allergic to fish, and I needed to stop eating fish and stop taking fish oil pills. The problem was embedded so deep within my system that even when I had stopped the symptoms continued for months.

I started taking allergy shots and had to leave work fifteen minutes early each day. The company would not allow me to come in fifteen minutes early or reduce my lunch hour by fifteen minutes, but told me I could no longer leave early for the allergy shots. I told this to the Lord in prayer and He solved my problem. Our New York Headquarters sent down a memo to their companies in Arizona stating that fifteen minutes would be knocked off our workday due to contract litigations. We would end our day at four o'clock rather than four-fifteen. I continue to take this to the Lord and in time he healed my body. **God works in mysterious ways!**

I had worked for the mines (ASARCO) during the summers while attending college. After graduating I was offered a job and worked for fifteen years before they decided to shut down. My initial requirement was a copy of my diploma indicating I had graduated from college. I worked there and even trained certain people who got the promotions that I never received. I moved from one position to another until I had learned most of the areas within the Accounting Department. Finally I was put in the position of head of the Accounts Payable Department.

After fifteen years the Copper Mines shut down. I had learned through time that I was the only Black working in the Department and I was also the only one that was required to have a college degree. The other employees in the accounting area were White and the most they had was a high school diploma. I went to my supervisor and asked him why I had not received a promotion in fifteen years, yet I was required to learn and work the different areas of accounting. His reply was they always thought I would be leaving at any time because I had a college degree.

I was angry and had nothing to lose so I asked, "At what point during those fifteen years did you realize I was going to stay?"

He put his head down showing his embarrassment. We both knew the real reason. Racism, prejudice and discrimination have a subtle way of showing its face in Tucson, Arizona. People are embarrassed and afraid to call you a Nigger to your face, so they say it in more subtle ways. Their mouth doesn't speak out, but their actions call you names. Many times I have gotten into an elevator with women of other persuasions than black, and they would move to the farthest point in the elevator and tightly hold on to their purse. The expressions on their faces were, because I was black, I was going to rob and/or rape her. I had white friends who would not speak to me in public, but on the job they were "mister and miss friendly." I also have friends that are not racist and did not discriminate against race, color or religion.

After leaving the mines I went to work for the Tucson Police Department for approximately fifteen years. I worked in Patrol for two years, a Special Task Force for three years, four years as a Gang Unit officer and four years as a School Resource Officer. I work in the areas of the city that were infested with drugs, prostitution and gang activity. For the fourteen-fifteen years I worked with the Department, I was always assigned to the same area of the city: Team 1. We also called this the Southside.

I think being a Black Man and having grown up in the Tucson area may have had some influence on my assignments. On April 30, 2000 I was medically retired due to injuries sustained on the Job, which resulted in two operations that left me with a forty percent disability on one knee and secondary damage to the other knee.

In retrospect, I look at my experience as an Officer as a blessing and an opportunity to have made a difference in the lives of many people. I also believe that the Supervisors and Commanders that were responsible for my assignments within each unit did the best thing and put me where I could be most effective.

I learned over the years that in the City of Tucson that both "good and bad people come in all colors." I have also learned that both "good and bad Police Officers came in one color, BLUE."

I believe that in each unit I worked, most of the officers were there to serve and to protect the public and to perform their duty to the best of their ability. But, there was always one in each unit that believed that the world revolved around them. They were self-centered, egotistical and vain. Their purpose was always the furtherance of their egos. I am thankful that I only met a few of these individuals during my tenor with the Department.

I believe that most of the officers come into the Department with the intent to do the right thing. They want to help in every way possible, but somewhere along the way, if they are not careful they become a part of the "Ass-Hole Syndrome."

This syndrome, as explained by our Behavior Science Personnel, is adopted by an officer who deduces through a series of events that the whole world is full of Ass Holes and he is the only sane person.

If I can paraphrase the concept as explained to me by a Behavioral Science expert, and be as succinct as possible, I shall do my best to explain this concept and how it comes about.

It begins like this: A novice police officer thinks and treats everyone as a good guy initially. The whole world is a bunch of good people struggling with the adversities of life. The same officer through a series of negative events comes to the conclusion after being on the job for a while that there are good guys and bad guys. The good guys are the Department he works with, fellow law officers and his family and friends. The bad guys are the public in general and they become known as ass-holes.

He later gets in a dispute with officers of another agency and due to this experience (s) he determines that all law enforcement officers other than his Department are ass-holes and puts them in the category with the general public.

He later gets into a disagreement with the Department. Perhaps he feels he got a bad deal or was treated unfairly and decides that the officers in his team, his family and friends are the good guys and the Department with a few exceptions is now in the "ass-hole category."

During several calls it appears the other units in the team are not performing to standard and perhaps his unit is the only hard working unit. He begins to sense a dissonance between his unit and the other units in the team. It could be competition in the field and he perceived his unit is being dumped on with numerous calls and other units are not doing their share of the call load. He then comes to the conclusion that his squad, his family and friends are the only good guys left and everyone else, including the other units in his team are now ass-holes.

He comes to work and finds himself over loaded with calls; his backup within his own unit appears to be asinine, leaving him to do most of the work day after day and the comradery of the unit has dissipated creating a schism in the unit. He now only trusts himself and can't get decent help even within his unit. He now determines that his unit is among the ass-holes and he stands alone in the whole Department.

He now believes that he is the only good guy on the Department, and the other good people are his family and friends. This starts to change when he continues to bring his work home; perhaps he starts drinking and fails at being a good spouse or parent. There is dissension in the home, pretty much due to his attitude and he feels now that his family and friends have taken sides against him. He becomes angry and treats his family and friends like criminals. He interrogates his children on family issues and is furious with his wife because she isn't there to back him up. His behavior alienates him from family and friends and he realizes that it's him against the world. Now it's him against all the ass-holes and he stands as the only sane person, yet in solitude.

He drinks more, comes home from work later each shift and tries to find understanding in another female in whom he found in the midst of all the ass-holes in the world. His job is now on the rocks, his marriage on the rocks and his drinks are the only thing not on the rocks. Now he is between a rock and a hard place and he leans to the drinks that are not on the rocks.

He now feels no one cares and if he left this world he wouldn't be missed. He is now at the final crossroads and he must choose between life and death. Without any help he will choose death and destruction, but with help he will choose to live.

We must understand that if you repent and are able to ask forgiveness and believe it, you will receive it. It is written, ***"For all have sinned and come short of the glory of God"*** **(Romans 3:23, KJV).** Christ said, ***"the thief (Satan) cometh not, but to steal, and to kill and to destroy: I am come that they might have life, and that they might have it more abundantly"*** **(John 10:10, KJV).**

To those of you that may be in the midst of the ass-hole syndrome seek the proper help and **the life you save may be your own.**

Chapter III
Field Training

Every Police Officer when he retires wishes he could have written down or documented his tour as a Police Officer. A Police Officer's life is a living book and every day is a different page or chapter. It is a book that can be labeled as drama, suspense, romance or even comedy, because life as a Police Officer is all those things.

I would like to tell you a few stories about each of the above listed labels. **Some of the language may not be suitable for younger children, due to actual quotes from those involved.**

I was a Minister in the church before I became an Officer and this seemed to pose a problem to those that were interviewing me on the oral boards. It also seemed to be a problem to the church, but since not one person from the church brought me a loaf of bread or a bag of beans to help support my family I thought it's better to listen to God and not man.

When the copper mines shut down many of us were jobless and I didn't know which way to turn. I prayed about the situation and promised God that whichever door he opened that's the one I would step in. At one point I was filling out an application and then next I was taking a test, and then I was getting a physical and on my way to the academy. It all seemed so sudden, except for the interruptions from the church folk who would come by with messages telling me "You "can't be a Minister and a Cop at the same time." I did notice though, they never brought any food for me or my family. Some of them didn't even have the nerves to tell me to my face, but they would send word by others saying you can't be a preacher and carry a gun. My response was, at least I have a badge and I'm certified to carry my gun.

God gave me the ability and the compassion to deal with people and at this moment in time this was the best way of doing it. It was more effective than preaching in the church. I was able to get out and see the world for what it really is, "a mess." I saw the people for what they really were, "sheep, lost sheep and goats." I brought more people to God on the job than I did while inside the church.

When you are dealing with church folk, it's different than dealing with the world. You would think that church folk would know better and they did. They just kept doing all the wrong things and would come and want you to tell them it was ok to lie, cheat and steal. I think the thing church folk steal the most is time. We come in late and we leave early; it seemed that in between we sleep or pass notes. We also have those folk that are always in bondage of some sort, either sickness or a bad situation. I believe that when this is constant in your life you either need to stop doing something or there is something you need to start doing. Whatever it is, it is keeping you from getting delivered.

I had a member that said he is ok in church until anyone starts bringing a message, and then he falls asleep. My advice to him was that Satan has a spirit that has taken away his joy and has blocked him from the word. He would never grow nor would he be able to survive without God's word. If he knew this and still allowed himself to come to church and go to sleep every time anyone brought a message, one day he would be held accountable for what he had missed. Satan has him sitting in the back so no one will notice him when he falls asleep. If that was a condition of mine, I would sit in the front row and have my friends to slap me in the face just to keep me awake and make the devil mad.

I prayed for this person and found out there were open doors in his life. Open doors are the opportunities that we give to Satan to come into our lives and take control. These doors are unlocked by weights and sins in our lives. I am reminded of the words of the Apostle Paul, *"Wherefore seeing we also are compassed about with so great a cloud of witnesses, let us lay aside every weight, and the sin which doth so easily beset us, and let us run with patience the race that is set before us, looking unto Jesus the author and finisher of our faith"* (Hebrews 12:1-2, KJV).

Yes, I do believe that God called me to be a Police Officer just as he called me to be a Minister. I touched more lives in one week as a Police Officer than I did in a year of preaching to the same people over and over again in the church.

A writer **(Sir Francis Day)** once said, *"I'd rather see a sermon than hear one, I'd rather you walk with me than just show me the way."* I desired to be a living epistle written by the hand of God on the hearts of everyone that I touched. I hope that someday when this life is over, someone will think of me and say, "He touched me."

I don't want to be remembered for achievements in education as Dr. King once said, or the merits received in sports, but as the words of a song that said,

> *If I can help somebody as I pass along,*
> *If I can cheer somebody with a word or a song,*
> *Then my living has not been in vain.*
> *If I can do my duty as a good man ought*
> *If I can bring back beauty to a world that is wrought*
> *And if I can spread God's message like the master taught,*
> *Then my living has not been in vain.*

When I got out of the Academy I had to go through a Field-Training Program. Here I learned that both men and women like people in uniform. I had numerous propositions during traffic stops and when reporting to calls. I can understand why some men concede to the temptations of the job. It doesn't matter how young or old you are, there is someone that will do anything to avoid a traffic citation or to avoid being arrested. They make sexual offers, they expose themselves; they offer financial bribes, and they have even offered me a better job if I didn't cite them or arrest them.

During the Field-Training Program I had the disappointment of having to ride with at least thirteen different officers during my training, because the Field Training Officers were not always available through the different phases. This was definitely a problem that needed correcting. Some of them were very astute while others were a poor excuse of a F.T.O. (Field Training Officer). I thank God that I was a Christian because some of their attitudes were deplorable. You have to understand that I was the only African American in the academy and the only one in the squad I was assigned to. My first week out, my Field Training Officer (FTO) introduced me to other Caucasian Officers while at a restaurant taking a break. Each of them shook my hand and introduced themselves by their first name. One female officer made it clear that I was not to call her by her first name. Only her friends could do that. She was to be referred to as Officer (?).

We talked for a while and it was clear to me after about four minutes that most of them were bigots. When a person of another race meets you and immediately starts telling you how not prejudice he is, then he is probably prejudice. When they start telling you that they have a Black friend like you or they know a Black family, they are probably bigots. An African American person does not want to know how many Black friends you have; a Mexican American does not want to know how many Mexican friends you have to make them comfortable. When I see a Caucasian officer, I don't immediately start telling him that I have White friends. When they demand that their first name is sergeant, lieutenant or captain, you still have a problem. If they talk to you as a person, never mentioning race and appear to be color blind, yet cognizant of all races and nationalities, you are probably dealing with a person that have learned to overcome culture biases.

I believe pride is as bad as being prejudice. The bible speaks of pride, as a sin God detest. Pride is a huge problem in law enforcement, but confidence is better than pride.

Cultural sensitivity was not taught at Tucson Police Department until years after I had become an officer. It was later taught by a friend of mine, Officer Boone. A good officer will notice that the person in front of him is African-American, Oriental, Native American, Mexican American or a Mexican from Mexico. This is very important because different cultures deal with issues differently. The character and behavior of people are often conducive of their culture and race. You must be cognizant of culture, different races or economical status of individuals. Everyone must be treated as individuals, fairly and appropriate.

Some of the F.T.O. personnel tried to denigrate me except for a couple. One officer in particular, I shall call officer **F**, a Hispanic male, seemed to know what I was going through. Perhaps he may have traveled down that road himself when he came on to the Department. But since nothing just happens, I believe God sent him. He took me for a few days and treated me like a person. He encouraged me when he said, "Just do what they say until you get on your on, then do it the best way you know how, especially if you know a better way." I remember him saying to me, "We brothers got to stick together." This was the turning point and after riding with him I was able to regain some strength and dignity and move on.

"F" was indeed a friend and a good officer. But to be honest with you, I think **F** missed his calling. He should have been a Black Comedian instead of a Mexican Police Officer. He had a way of cheering you up and it kept you laughing the hold time you were around him. The only problem with **F** is that he would have you laughing so hard that when you went on a call, he would be serious, but you were still cracking up from his previous comedy act and the people would think YOU were crazy. **"F"** would have me laughing so hard I had tears in my eyes. You would have to walk away so they wouldn't see the tears, which were brought on by **F** talking like Daffy Duck, Porky Pig or Elmer Fudd.

Sometimes he would have a toy that sounded like someone passing gas and would use it at the most inappropriate time. He would be careful who he chose to entertain. Usually right after you had gained your composure and put on your serious face, then would come the fake farting.

He would say with a heavy Mexican accent, "Excuse me sir, it must be the frijoles (beans) I had for lunch."

He would then continue pretending to pass gas using the concealed little toy as though he had no control. The person he was talking with would try to move away from him for fear of the odor. Eventually **F** would reveal his secret to them. The person would say, "I noticed I didn't smell anything," and we all would laughed together. He seemed to know who to use it on and when.

I had an FTO who I shall call Pal, who seemed to be very knowledgeable. We seem to respond to all the gruesome calls, like homicides, suicides, fatal traffic accidents, and etc. He seemed to enjoy explaining to me that the gray matter on the pavement was brain matter. We rolled up on several individuals who had been killed in a homicide and it gave him great pleasure to look at the bodies and analyze the situation that got them there.

On one occasion we found a man that had been beaten to death. The officer was very descriptive in pointing out the gruesome details of the wounds.

"Take a look at this wound," he said, "how deep do you think it is? Man, I know he felt that."

On another occasion we arrived on the scene of a pedestrian who had been killed while crossing the street. Pal wanted me to pay close attention to the shoe that had been knocked off the foot of the victim and the laces were still tied. He proceeded to inform me how the body relaxes at death and often the last thing that happens is the release of fluids and bowel movement.

We went to several suicide attempts and he would say, "These people don't know how to commit suicide the right way. If you're going to do it, you should do it right."

He told me once: "I went to a suicide call one day, and the lady had shot herself in the head with a shotgun. When I got there she was laying on the couch with half her face blown off. I examined her visually and made the comment, 'damn, you sure made a mess of this.' I almost pissed my pants," he replied, "when she responded, "Is it that bad?""

"I thought she was dead, but she had survived with half of her face missing," he said. "She couldn't even do it properly with a shotgun."

We later went to a suicide attempt where a lady had attempted suicide by means of cutting her wrist and then called her estranged husband to say goodbye.

Pal stated, "Just another person pretending that she wants to die."

"What do you mean pretending," I asked?

"If she wanted to die do you think she would have called someone," he stated? "No, these people don't know what they're doing and most of them are glad they don't. If you're going to do it, you might as well do it right."

"Do you know how to do it right," I asked?

"Yes, I do," he replied, as if he was glad I asked. "If you're really going to do it, you have to make sure it's going to be fatal. Take a revolver and open your mouth and shoot upward through the brain. I doubt if you would feel a thing."

"How would you know unless you tried," I responded?

"Well, if you take out the brains you shouldn't feel anything," he said.

I responded, "But it is the brain that sends signals and pulses that lets us know about pain. Perhaps it may be the most painful way."

"No," he retorted, "just do what I said if you want to be successful."

Before getting out of the program, we responded to a call of a D.O.A. (dead on arrival) at home. When we arrived we went in to see the victim and try and make a determination if death was of natural causes. Pal lifted the sheets to view the body and quickly froze in his tracks. It didn't appear anyone was in the room with us and he whispered, "You gotta see this!"

I walked over to where he was standing and looked under the lifted sheet. It was a little boy whose limbs were deformed. His body was shaped like a dog like animal and he was lying on his side. The small body was covered with blotches of hair and his face was wrinkled. He had facial hair on the sides of his cheeks and he appeared to be at peace. We were so shocked by what we were seeing that we were totally oblivious to the fact that someone was watching.

"He was a good boy and when he was born the doctors only gave him a few weeks to live," interrupted a female voice from the doorway. "He could only lie on his side and be comfortable, so when they put him in the casket, I want him to be on his side."

I was too embarrassed to ask her about the boy's shape and features, but it was apparent he was an oddity. We completed our report and the young boy was taken to the appropriate mortuary. Afterwards we both looked at each other in disbelief saying, "What was that?"

In the final days of the program, Pal and I responded to an accidental death of a teenage boy. Apparently they said a gun had gone off, but when dealing with the Mexican Nationals on that particular side of town you never really know what happened. There were hits being made by drug dealers from across the border, and Tucson was only an hour's drive from Mexico. It seems that when the aliens come across the border everyone forgets how to speak English and many become deaf and dumb. The case was turned over to the detectives and we were on our way to another call.

Pal was full of police stories and didn't mind telling you and didn't leave out any of the horrific gruesome bloody details.

Once he said, "I went on a call to that house," pointing to the house of an acquaintance that had died in the house. He never knew that I knew the family and I didn't tell him. I had heard that the young man had died, but no one gave any details. I was curious to hear his explanation.

He continued, "We went into the home and the house was dark. There was a guy sitting on the couch with a bag over his head and his fingers resting on his stomach. We drew our weapons and surrounded him, but there was no movement. After backing the dog down that was inside and allowing him to run out of the room we turned the lights on. There sitting on a couch was a Black male with a paper bag over his head. We moved the bag from his head and discovered that both eyeballs had been pulled from the sockets and hanging down. His hand was indeed on his stomach, but he had cut himself open and had been playing with his intestines before he died. The reason the dog was so obstinate about leaving is because he had been locked in the room and had gotten so hungry he started to feed on the dead body. Initially the dog had gnawed away on the couch where blood had splattered, then after a day or two he started gnawing on the victim. Apparently the subject had taken PCP and mutilated himself after overdosing."

I never told Pal that I knew the victim's family. Perhaps it would have stopped him from telling the story, but I doubt it.

We went to a suicide call where someone had shot himself in the head. It wasn't our call, we just responded. After we had left the scene Pal blurted out, "Yeah, finally someone who knew what they were doing!"

Later on in my career I was told that Pal had been promoted to sergeant. He had gotten involved in a domestic situation and could possibly be demoted. When officers responded to his home he took his weapon and committed suicide. He did it exactly the way he had recommended to me years earlier. Perhaps his obsession with death and suicide prepared him for his final task.

It's happening all over this Country. Officers in fear of losing their job, rank, family and homes are taking their lives. We all have stories of Police Officers that took their lives.

I had a friend and his wife was involved with an officer from another agency. **I will not say what State or what Department of Law Enforcement he was in.**

He made several attempts to go to the other agency hoping they could talk to the other party and remind him of his breach of morals and ethics, but nothing was done. He was told there was nothing they could do, because it was a civil problem. She had taken the kids, and after some obvious encounters of seeing her with the other person, he lost it. He went to Benefits and asked if his children would be able to get the money if he committed suicide. They said, "Yes," so the next day he went to her and called her to come out. When she came out, he said, "you have taking everything, you might as well have it all" (reference to his children and the money). He shot himself in front of her.

We are involved in spiritual warfare and Satan is the enemy. He is a liar and a thief and the bible tells us: **The thief cometh not but to steal, and to kill and to destroy..." (John 10:10, KJV).**

The spirit of suicide is a spirit that overwhelms police officers. It is a spirit of hopelessness and emptiness, and it convinces you its best not to go on, because there is nothing for you beyond that moment. This spirit tells you that by taking your life you can punish those you leave behind or you can punish the world for neglecting you or by erasing yourself it solves all your problems. Satan has taken up a stronghold in your mind and his ultimate goal is to kill and destroy. When praying for my fellow officers, I pray against this spirit. I believe officers have such high standards and values, that when they cross the line in some way or another, they feel so guilty they believe they are punishing themselves for what they believe to be an unforgivable breach of morals, ethics and character. They may also feel they are at a point of no return. The very thought of losing their job; being demoted or having a problem they cannot fix is unacceptable. I believe that it is associated with the spirit of pride and the spirit of pride seems to be at the root of most sins.

When someone whom you never expected to do such a thing does just that, it is hard to accept. When a fellow officer is devastated, he thinks about the officer that took his life and believes he has just as much right to kill himself. I believe the more people that commit suicide on the force, the more it fuels the temptation and it gets easier for others to justify themselves. It becomes an easy way out for many officers, but they need to realize that the second after they pulled that trigger they will find themselves in their eternal destination. Hell and not paradise will most likely be their domain. I believe self murder is a sin in most cases. Since there is no time in death, the moment you pull that trigger or leave this world you stand before your maker.

That act of murder or self murder is to make the person disappear. Many officers just want to disappear, so they erase themselves.

We must understand that the three avenues of sin are: **the flesh, the world and the Devil.** The Apostle John talks about pride as a source of sin. He says, *"for all that is in the world, the lust of the flesh, and the lust of the eyes, and the pride of life, is not of the father, but is of the world"* **(1John 2:16, KJV).**

I have come to the conclusion that most officers have problems, because they are unbalanced. Job said, *"Let me be weighed in an even balance that God may know mine integrity"* **(Job 31:6, KJV).** In the book of Daniel it is said, *"... Thou art weighed in the balance, and art found wanting"* **(Daniel 5:27, KJV).** The instability of some officers is because they have been *"weighed in the balance and art found wanting."*

We as people must understand, you can't fill a spiritual void with material things. Not having Christ as the priority in our lives created a void, and not having Christ at all creates an emptiness that can not be filled with natural or material things.

Officers often put too much weight on their job and their relationship with other officers and little weight on their spiritual life, their families and their health. Pride is a big part of the equation as to why many self-destruct. Pride, arrogance, self-centeredness, being egotistical and the know-it-all syndrome are part of an equation for many Police Officers who commit self-murder. These factors can only be eliminated by God and without God your formula equals to disaster.

I have met very few officers on the force that didn't have an issue with pride. It is almost impossible to instruct a proud and arrogant person and it is almost impossible for them to receive criticism. Scriptures tells us that it is dangerous to have a heart filled with pride.

- *"When pride cometh, then cometh shame..."* **(KJV Proverbs 11:2).**
- *"Pride goeth before destruction and a haughty spirit before a fall..."* **(KJV Proverbs 16:18).**

I believe there is more power in having temperance and being humble than in being proud and arrogant. A proud man cannot restrain himself, and he or she acts often without thinking. Therefore, a proud officer will find himself before a board for disciplinary actions if he or she isn't careful.

The question that many ask is: can you be an effective police officer without having a since of pride? The answer is yes, because what a police officer needs to be is confident. Confidence is what the Department is looking for not pride or arrogance. Confidence comes from having the knowledge and ability to do the job. Pride is being more into self and it is saying to everyone, "Look at me!" Confidence says, "I can do it," and confidence comes from being astute, well trained and informed. We need to stop preaching pride and give our officers the tools to be confident.

Paul writes: *"For I say, through the grace given unto me, to every man that is among you, not to think of himself more highly than he ought to think..."* **(KJV, Romans 12:3).** We also read, *"The patient in spirit is better than the proud in spirit"* **(KJV, Ecclesiastes 7:8).**

Officers should learn that we can help each other, but only after we move the chip from our shoulder. The Apostle Peter said, *"be subject one to another, and be clothed with humility: for God resisteth the proud, and giveth grace to the humble"* **(KJV, 1 Peter 5:5).**

I have gotten more information from suspects and victims by just being nice. It's just nice to be nice. If you are humble you have God on your side. Being humble does not mean you are weak. Meekness is power under control. It takes a strong person to have temperance and humility. I would rather be humble and receive God's grace, than to be proud and praised by the Devil.

The job (Law Enforcement) becomes so endowed in officers that their nomenclature remains the same even at home or around family and friends. You can't talk to your family using the same language and terminology you use on the job and expect them to understand and say, "10-4" after every statement. Codes are often different, but these are some Examples:

1. The wife calls you to do something and your response is, **"I'm 10-6" (busy) can I "45" (meet) with you later?**

2. You come home and tell your wife, **"The reason I am late is because I had to respond to a 10-43 (Robbery) and the other members had already went 10-7 (out of service)."**

3. Your children are having a sibling dispute and you tell them, **"If I have to take command of this situation I will find out who the suspect is and who the victim is. When I do there won't be a hearing, so you better plead guilty and don't even attempt to give a false statement."**

4. Your neighbor comes over and discovers you have a new television. Your response is, "Yeah after being on the front line for many years it went 10-7 **(out of service).** My family was upset but when I said we could get another one, the situation became "code 4" **(ok).** I transported my family to the 10-20 (location) to retrieve another and when we were 10-23 **(arrive at location)** at the 10-20 **(location)** we observe the set we wanted. It was 10-8 **(in service or on)** in the Northwest quad of the building resting independently on a shelf. After questioning the salesman we signed the proper documents and exited the premises. While 10-18 **(en route)** to our code 11 **(home)** we took a 10-10 **(break)** but it turned into a code 7 **(lunch).** Finally we were 10-18 **(en route)** and went 10-23 **(arrive at location)** at our code 11 **(residence)** within minutes. There she is and it has been 10-8 **(in service)** ever since." Officers should learn when to turn it on and when to shut it off.

Chapter IV
Tilted

When your job outweighs your family you have just become unbalanced or shall I say tilted. When your priorities are off, you become unbalanced, or shall I say tilted? The first order of priority should be your relationship with God, your family and then your job.

The reason I say tilted is because it means to cause to "slope, slant or lean." You must be upright in all your dealings with family, friends and on the job. When I was a child playing at the penny arcades I would put my money in the pinball machine. I would pull the lever to propel the little ball out and it would hit different obstacles within the machine causing me to get points. Some times I would help it a little and shake the machine. The consequence for this action would be the machine would shut down. Before it shut down it would light up with a message that said, "TILTED."

Many officers are walking around with the message TILTED on their foreheads. This means the machine is about to shut down. When you see your fellow officer with the tilted sign you should heed the warning. Speak first to the officer, and if you are unable to succeed, talk to someone that can.

Help for officers should be made more readily accessible. I believe help should go to the officer and not wait for the problem person to come to the help. Many of them will not take that step because of pride and the embarrassment of others finding out about it.

The only time that Behavior Science Personnel come to you is when a drastic situation has already occurred. Showing up after an incident or after the suicide is not the answer. We are taught as officers to be proactive. Why won't the Department be proactive in helping their own?

I believe every officer should have an appointment to talk to Behavior Science Personnel at least twice a year. They should do this just to check basis with the officers. The proper questions and the proper interview techniques may result in you being able to detect if someone is tilted and about to shut down. The cost to do this does not compare to the loss of a life. The Behavior Science Unit should be open to officers with degrees in the helping fields (counseling, psychology, social science, etc.). Have a field unit that can go out into the field and talk with officers with problems, perhaps do a ride along for a short period of time (couple of hours, or part of a day).

Preliminary signs of dysfunction can be found in every officer with a problem. Every officer that has taken his life or had to be dismissed because of inappropriate actions left some previous signs along the way. Someone may not have taken them serious, but the signs were there. You may have even thought that if this person can command a unit or a team of officers, surely he or she can resolve their family issues. That indeed is wrong and may prove to be a fatal assumption.

Law Enforcement Officers are committing suicide at an alarming rate. The problems that causes a person to take their life is not a natural problem, it is spiritual. A natural mask covers what appear to be of a natural origin but in reality the problem is spiritual. **You can't resolve a spiritual problem with a natural solution.** It's like putting a band aide on a severed limb to stop the bleeding. You can have all the worldly counseling, go to all the meetings, and attend all the classes afforded to you, but if they are not spiritually balanced you will continue having the same results: domestic disputes, and suicides or self murder. **You can't fill a spiritual void with natural things.** If a person has a broken heart for losing a love one through divorce or abandonment, you can't fill the void in their heart by giving them a bigger home, a newer car or more money.

There are three major areas that should be of great concerned to Law Enforcement: Relationships, Finances and Job Stress.

- **Relationships:** Being a police officer has a tremendous affect on those that are married and with family. Uniforms attract certain people. In fact, both men and women will tell you they like a person in uniform. When officers are on call they meet people, when they patrol their respective beats they meet people, when they are assigned to certain projects they meet people. There are many temptations that come your way and there are other situations you create yourself if you're not careful. You must spend time with your family and stop using your spouse as a garbage dump. Take on some responsibilities with your family and not push it off on your spouse. You should be the priest in your own home. Work on being a good husband and a good father or a good wife and a good mother. Outings with other officers are not designed to give you the proper rest and relaxation you would receive by being with your family. Hopefully the Department will one day make it possible for you to attend classes with your spouse concerning marriage and family relations.

- **Finances:** Police Officers are guilty of having the "Keep up with the Jones' Syndrome." They think they should all have new houses, a new car, a macho truck and they compete to see who can have the most toys. In order to do this you have to work all the overtime you can and keep your name on the off duty work list constantly. Most of them are in dire need of financial and budgeting advice (counseling). Too many divorces can drain you of your income, so concentrate on keeping your marriage together and on supporting one spouse. Scripture tells us that Satan's avenues of temptation are *"the lust of the flesh, the lust of the eyes and the pride of life."* You don't have to have every thing you want, everything you see and everything you think will make you a status symbol. Your manhood is not determined by how big your truck is or how many square feet your house is built on. It is ones ability to righteously provide for his family and to love them unconditionally that defines the man.

- **Job Stress:** A police officer will make as much as ten to fifteen contacts a day. Each time contact is made the adrenaline rush kicks in. Every traffic stop or encounter has the potential to take the officer's life, so officers prepare themselves by getting up for the possible situation; much like one would psyche themselves up for a game. When the situation is over the adrenaline has to exit the body somehow or be absorbed. Perhaps through jumping calls, foot patrol, having a temper tantrum and going off on a suspect; victim, another officer or a family member when you get home. All day long you have had adrenaline rushes and you have been high and low through out the day. When you get home after work you are either too high to get involved with the family because everyone is moving too slow for you or you're too low which means you don't want to be bothered, and you're the one moving too slow and you just want to rest. If you're not careful you find out that having a few drinks seems to help. Then you need more help, which means more drinks. Soon there are not enough hours in the day to do your job and be a good parent and a good mate. There is not enough money to do the things you want and you find out that you can better relate to others than you can with your wife and kids. They simply don't understand you. While making a few stops and going to a few calls or perhaps while just doing your normal daily routine, you find someone that better understands you. This creates a marital problem and when you are faced with the reality of losing the ones you love because of you not being able to keep your relationship going with your family, or that you are going to lose your house and your toys because you failed at being a good steward over your finances, or the stress of the job have brought about drinking problems and attitude problems in your life that now no one wants to be around you, you have the perfect solution to punish them all. Why not, they won't miss you anyway, because while you're alive no one seemed to care. Satan is now in charge and he has endowed in your mind and heart the spirit of suicide or self murder. Now is the time to decide: should I or should I not take my life? God has seen your situation and he has sent angels to help you to fight against the spirits of evil. You now have to make a decision because the choice is yours. What you have here is a person that has become TILTED.

I had a friend on the Department that was always involved in domestic disputes with his wife. He brought much of it on himself by trying to have a sweetheart and a wife at the same time. He would come to work sober and alert, but he would tell me about his drinking and his adulterous acts. My Sergeant and I would talk to him about his situation. The Sergeant who was a person who cared about his people would call him in and ask how things were going.

One day the Officer called me on the radio and asked me to meet him. I was on a traffic stop and told him to meet me at that location. When he arrived he said, "I need to talk to you!"

"Is it urgent," I responded? "I didn't want to be interrupted at that moment."

He took his index finger and put it in his mouth and with his thumb he simulated a hammer of a pistol and pretended to shoot himself in the mouth. At that point I dismissed the person on the traffic stop and immediately took the time to talk with him. I encouraged him and told him about the one person that could truly help him and that was Jesus Christ. I also let him know that I loved him as person and would be there if he needed. Afterwards he told me, "that is what I really needed, not Behavior Science, not counselors or psychiatrist but to know that someone cares and that Jesus loves me."

Sometimes people don't need you to solve their problems, they just want to be guided in the right direction and to know that someone cares. Sometimes it's just a listening ear or a word of encouragement that can save a life.

I didn't try to manipulate the blame in his situation nor did I belittle the seriousness of his ordeal. I did remind him that troubles don't last always, and if he would give God the chance he would not regret it. I reminded him of the scripture that said, *"...weeping may endure for a night, but joy cometh in the morning"* **(Psalms 30:2, KJV)**.

He had tears in his eyes, and when I said to him, "Hey, I love you man." He started laughing and said, "I really believe you do and thanks." He came to me in turmoil and he left with peace of mind. It was as Peter said in the scripture **(Acts 3:6)**, *"silver and gold have I done, but such as I have I give unto thee."*

I made him promise to do what I had suggested in our conversation and we would get together the next morning. I had given him some sound advice on dealing with his situation at home and convinced him to adhere to an agreement with me. He committed to our agreement and it gave him more time. Sometimes all a potential victim needs is to get beyond the moment.

A few weeks later we were having lunch together and he brought up that day when he asked for help. He said at that moment if he had not found me he would have ended his life.

I advised him that if he had the opportunity to be there for someone else, don't hesitate. I remember telling him that life is a puzzle and God knows where all the pieces fit, but God's ways are not our ways and His thoughts are not our thoughts.

"When you put a puzzle together," I said. "Where do you start?"

"With the corners," he replied, "or I find all the pieces with a straight side to fit around the edges or I match up the colors?"

"Well," I said, "when God began to put together the pieces of the puzzle to your life, he can place them any where on the board, because he knows where all the pieces go."

"So when things are going on in my life, God is putting down pieces of the puzzle in the right places," he remarked, "even when they don't make sense?"

"Yes," I said, "and they don't always connect at that moment, but somewhere along the way the puzzles will come together. But you have to trust Him."

He laughed and said, "Brother, some of those pieces are so far apart I wonder if they will ever come together?"

A few days later I called him to meet me and he did. When he arrived in his vehicle I rolled down my window and asked, "How's my brother? He gestured as if he had pieces of a puzzles in his hand and he kissed the alleged puzzles. Then he pretended to place the puzzles on difference spots on his car dash as if it was the puzzle board.

He gave me a big smile before he said a word. "He's still putting the puzzles down and every once in a while they connect," he replied. "Every now and then it makes sense."

"Good," I said, "so don't panic if one doesn't connect right away."
He gave me the thumbs up gesture and drove away.

My friend was an officer that was tilted. I didn't solve all his problems, but I was there during a critical moment, which may have saved his life.

Alcohol was a big problem in the life of my friend, as well as other officers. The following exerts were taken from a news article:

"An interesting problem among officers is alcohol abuse. Alcoholism when mixed with policing is very dangerous. Officers feeling stressed out on the job and feel that a way to relieve this stress is to stop at a bar and have a drink or have what they call "choir practice" with their buddies. They have a special meeting place, secluded and convenient for the unit or a group to come together after a shift. Whether it is beer or hard liquor, it can become an addicting routine.

Excessive drinking creates a communication barrier between husband and wife, and the user and their children. Conflict resolution is to resolve a problem without creating a new problem. Alcohol may cause you to temporarily forget the problem, but it returns when you're sober again. It doesn't solve the problem, it creates a new problems.

The stress of daily life, coupled with stresses from tragic events, can push a police officer to end his life. Robert Douglas, executive director of the National P.O.L.I.C.E. Suicide Foundation states, "We are losing about 300 officers a year to suicide---" (Fields and Jones, 1999).

One forensic psychologist Cindy Goss of New York listed the following as a profile typical of a police suicide: "The cop who commits suicide is a male, white, 35, working patrol, abusing alcohol, separated or seeking a divorce, experiencing a recent loss or disappointment. Typically domestic abuse is involved (Loh, 1994). *Also, about 90 percent of the time the cop is drinking heavily when he shoots himself* (Loh, 1994).

The officer who brings the stress of the job home seems most at risk. A suicidal police officer may fear suicide but they may fear life just as much. Especially as the rationalizations, denials, and excuses crumble, the officer is left with the spectacle of his or her wasted and broken life (Milam and Ketcham, 1981).

Most police officers witness some of life's most horrible scenes. The following will list examples of traumatic events (National Center For PTSD, 1999):
· *Life-threatening danger or physical harm*
· *Exposure to gruesome death, bodily injury or bodies*
· *Extreme environmental or human violence or destruction*
· *Extended exposure to danger, loss or emotional/physical strain -- extreme fatigue, weather exposure, hunger or sleep deprivation.*

Further, the American Counseling Association lends that PTSD can surface several weeks, months, or years after the exposure to the event. Depression is one symptom and the following are examples of other PTSD symptoms (American Counseling Association, 1999):
· *Re-experiencing the event through memories, flashbacks, or dreams*
· *Crying uncontrollably*
· *Fear and sense of doom about the future*
· *Suicidal idealization*

Cindy Goss advised, "Cops are controlling individuals" (Loh, 1994); *therefore, any one or any combination of the examples of the symptoms above can leave a police officer feeling totally out of control. As a reminder, the provided list above is only a few examples of the symptoms that can be associated with PTSD.*

In conclusion, police officers are killing themselves at a rate more than twice as high as the general public (McNamara, 1996). *The fact is that virtually all suicides caused by depression and anger is preventable with appropriate intervention* (Brown, 1998).

On July 28, 1999, Surgeon General David Satcher states, "suicide is the eighth leading cause of death in the United States, claiming about 30,000 lives in 1997, compared with fewer than 19,000 homicides" (Huntsville Times, 1999). *It is obvious that prevention, education and training must be paramount in all departmental training.*

Departments must stop ignoring the problem before the problem becomes a nightmare. Too many excellent and proficient police officers have ended their life when perhaps help was only a call away. Police departments need to confront the stress of the job before the sound of Taps can be heard once again shrieking from

31

a police officer's gravesite" **(Every police Department's Nightmare: Officer Suicide by SGT Monroe Dugdale, 1 August 99).**

These figures were calculated eleven years ago and at the time the problem was on the increase.

Being a Police Officer was very rewarding for me because I had a life outside of the Department. That is also a remedy for some of the problems that officers have. **I recommend that you have a life outside of the Department and with friends that are not Police Officers. Go out and be with people that do not speak to you in the "ten codes" or use police nomenclature. Allow your mind and your spirit to take a break from the culture itself.**

I believe the whole time I was on the Force God protected me and made me available for others. I had the chance to witness to and help more people in one day while on patrol than I did in one month as a pastor in the church.

I would like to share with you some of those cases, but let me remind you that some of the actual language used is based on actual quotes and may not be appropriate for children. The names have been changed to protect the guilty, because if they were innocent they wouldn't mind.

Chapter V: Patrol
Case 1: Number Six (Mental)

I had gotten out of the F.T.O. Program and was on my own when I met Scott from another team. The frequency was opened, and I responded to a call in another team for a back up. Someone had allegedly tried to set an elderly lady's house on fire. When I arrived it was obvious that this lady was a "Number Six" (that meant that she had mental problems). Scott was a Caucasian male and he was my backup and never said much except he laughed at what was going on between me and the elderly white lady. I think he had been there previously and knew the complainant.

She told me that she didn't like Black people and wondered if I knew any. I told her I had some friends that were Black but I wouldn't trust them if I was her. She was an elderly lady and I don't think she even noticed that I was Black. She was so focused on her prejudice that she was blinded by the fact that I was being very nice and understanding. Kindness and compassion will blind people who are racist, but it must be given to them in large doses. Since I was a nice person and seemed to comprehend her dilemma, there was no way that her conscious mind would see me as a Black man. If she accepted me as a Black officer then all her up bringing about mean nasty niggers would be invalid. Her concepts were absolute so the possibility of the existence of one nice Blackman would destroy her infallible perception of Blacks, so, as for as she was concerned I was a White officer.

"These Blacks are always coming over and setting my house on fire," she said. "Come with me and I will show you."

We walked around the house and there was nothing. She would show me a stick on the ground or a small stone and say, "they threw these at my house."

It was apparent that the rocks and other debris she showed me had been there for quite some time.

"So you know some Black people," she said, thinking about what I had said minutes ago.

"Yes maam. You know they called them Niggers where I come from," I said, pretending to talk in a low voice so no one could hear. "I'm trying to learn more about them so we can get rid of the ones in our neighborhood," I whispered; again giving her the impression that we were not to let Scott hear us since she have perceived him to be Black.

"Did you know that they all ate watermelon and chicken," I stated, continuing the conversation?

"I heard that," she replied. "Is there any on the Police Department?"

At that point Scott interrupted, "what's wrong with watermelon and chicken? I like watermelon and chicken."

"You see maam," I said, "I believe we have one of those Negroes here pretending to be a White man," referring to Scott.

She beckoned me with one finger and entreated me to bend down so she could whisper to me in private. She didn't want Scott to hear.

"Damn," she said. "They're everywhere son, you better be careful with this one," implying that Scott could be a problem.

"I'm not worried maam; if he's trying to pretend to be White he's just trying to cross over. They're what we call an Uncle Tom." I said loud enough for Scott to hear.

It wasn't long before I convinced her that Scott was a Black man and I was White. Scott was laughing aloud as he shined his light on me so the lady could see, but it didn't matter to her.

"Damn Nigger," she said referring to Scott. She was angry that he had shined his light on me. "That will make him a target for the other niggers in the neighborhood," she commented with a nervous voice.

"Like I said before maam," I belted, "they're out of control. Next he will be trying to buy a house right next to yours. He will then throw watermelon seeds and chicken bones all over your yard."

"Ain't that the truth? Can't you do something about that," the little lady said sadly as she looked to me for help?

"I'll talk to my supervisor about it maam. Maybe we can turn them around before they get here."

"Good Lord I hope so!" she responded.

I looked her in the eyes and said, "Maam if there is nothing else, then I'll take this nigger and leave."

"Thank you son," she said, "you're such a good boy."

"There is only a few of us left maam, and we need your prayers," I said as I shook her hand and slowly walked away with Scott who was laughing hysterically.

Scott and I became friends and for a moment he became Black and I was a White boy. Thanks to a little old bigot lady who couldn't tell the difference between a Black man and a White man.

Case 2A: Angel or Transient-1

I had just gotten through training and I made a vow that I would do a good deed each day that I worked. I did foot patrol at a park called Santa Rita Park and as I drove by I would see this old Blackman pushing a shopping cart. He had hoary hair and appeared to be a loner. He had the appearance that he was hungry and hadn't eaten for days. Each day I was drawn to him and he would show up at various places on my beat. A voice said, *There goes an opportunity to do a good deed.* I thought to myself, *"why this guy?"*

I saw him at the park the following day and decided to stop. When I approached him he reached out his hand, but he never said a word. I took all the money I had in my pocket and gave it to him, about seven dollars. He took the money as if he was waiting for me and continued walking and pushing his cart. He then slowly pushed his cart to the farthest part of the park from where we were standing. I turned and took a couple of steps towards my car, then turned to see where he was and he had disappeared. I had felt strange while in his presence, but thought it was the warmth of the sun shining on me directly.

The next day I was drawn to the park again. This time I thought, *"If I see this guy I'm not giving him anything."* As I approached the park, there he was standing alone with his cart. I exited my vehicle and approached him. I was determined to find out who he was. As I came into his presence he reached out his hand and I was overwhelmed with sadness. It was as though he was the epitome of adversity and represented every homeless person in the world. I reached into my pocket and gave him all that I had. He never said a word but walked away pushing his cart. I returned to my vehicle and when I came to myself I was about to drive away.

"No way," I said aloud. "I'm going to run this guy through the computer and find out who he is."

I drove around the park and he could not be located. When I ask other transients who he was, they said they never saw the guy. I didn't know if they were apprehensive because of the uniform or trying to be loyal to one of their own or if they were telling the truth.

One guy responded, "I saw you over there talking to yourself. I thought for a moment you had lost it!"

"You didn't see the old Black guy with me," I blurted out?

"No sir Officer," he replied. "I just saw you over yonder sticking your hand out in front of you and talking to yourself."

The third day I was determined to find this guy and run him through the computer and find out something about him. I drove around taking calls and at the end of the day I spotted him standing in the dessert area. I drove right up to where he was standing and walked up to him.

"I don't know who you are but the Lord must like you because I keep giving you all my money but that is going to stop!" I yelled.

As I was talking he reached out his hand and I couldn't speak. Again I was overwhelmed by sadness and even a sense of grief. I reached into my pocket and gave him ten dollars, which was all the money I had. Immediately he looked at me with tears in his eyes. I could see that his eyes were very sad and that he could see through my feigned anger.

"Thank you sir, thank you sir, thank you sir," he said in a soft, shaky, but pleasant voice. It was as though he was thanking me for all three days at once.

As I stood there he walked away as though he had accomplished his mission. I stood and watched, as he appeared to dissipate in the distance. For the next few days I search for him and couldn't find him. I was eating my lunch in the park hoping he would show up, but he never did. I opened my bible and started to read as I ate my lunch.

The pages of the bible fell open to a certain part. It was **Hebrews 13:1-2** and it read, *"Let brotherly love continue. Be not forgetful to entertain strangers: for thereby some have entertained angels unawares."*

Case 2B: Angel or Transient-2

I had met a guy that told me he had bought him a pass from the city and his ID cost him $19.25. He showed me he had the money, but wanted me to give him a dollar for a cup of coffee.

"No problem," I said, and I gave him a couple of bucks and he went into the convenience store and bought himself a cup of coffee like he had said.

I was off work the next day so I took my son to the gym to workout. I told him about the incident with the transient who I had given money to on several occasions and that I was convinced he was an angel. He had a hard time believing me. I told him that the bible said to be careful how you entertain people because you could be talking to an angel **("be not forgetful to entertain strangers for thereby some have entertained angels unawares," Hebrews 13:2).**

After the workout we stopped at a Circle K to get a drink, and of course there were transients hanging out waiting for a hand out.

"I'm sure if that happened to me dad," he said, "I would know if it's an angel or not."

There was one guy who looked clean and he was African American and he came to us. Of course we expected it, so we just waited for him to give his speech.

"Hi sir," he said, "I know you hear this all the time but I would appreciate if one of you brothers could give me a few dollars for a city ID. I have a job interview and if I can't show them an ID, they won't interview me."

I knew how much it cost from talking to the guy the day before who said he had $19.25 for his ID, but needed a dollar for a cup of coffee.

"I'm just asking for a little to help me out," He pleaded, "I'm not asking for all the money."

I knew he was lying and probably didn't even know how much an ID cost. I asked him, knowing I would catch him in a lie, "how much does it cost for an ID card?"

He looked at me and my grandson and smiled as he stated, "$19.25 Sir, I believe its $19.25.

My grandson gave me the look that he didn't have that kind of money, so I gave the guy a $20 dollar bill, since he had the correct answer.

He asked me if I wanted him to go inside and get change, but I said no. I knew that it cost $19.25 and he could just keep the change.

"Thank you Sir, I really appreciate you helping a brother out," he said with a smile."

The guy left walking through an open field towards the city and had only gone about twenty yards, when my grandson asked me if I felt strange while talking to the man.

I thought he was feeling sorry for the guy, so I said, "you want me to give him a ride?"

When we looked in the direction he had started walking, he had vanished. We both exited the vehicle and looked again in the direction he had gone. There was no way he could cover a distance of a couple hundred yards in a few seconds. He was not in the store and it had been less than a minute since we talked with him.

I remembered what he had said about feeling strange, so I asked him what he meant. He said, "I just felt weird when I was near him."

It all happened so fast that I didn't know what to say. My grandson then whispered to me, "**be not forgetful to entertain strangers for thereby some have entertained angels unawares**. Now I believe," he said, "now I believe."

Case 3: "Nigger, there ain't no God!"

It was a cold and dreary day in the middle of an unusual winter for Tucson. It was raining and I was working the night shift. We had a status called "Deep Freeze." It meant that if the temperatures dropped below freezing certain shelters would be open for the homeless or less unfortunate individual that didn't have a place to go.

Police officers were expected to help those less fortunate and arrange to get them to specific shelters or make them aware of such places. It was indeed an act of kindness that some Cops thought it beneath their dignity. Usually those who thought that way had no compassion or dignity in the first place.

It is sad that many Cops who claim to be Christians hide in the closets of life afraid they will be ridiculed. I wanted people in the Department and out of the Department to know there was something genuinely different about me. I think it is an insult to God for Christians to live in this world and people never know you are a Christian. There are many people who claimed salvation through Christ, but "if they were arrested for being a Christian would they be found not guilty." I do not believe God delights in secret members; our relationship with Christ should be open to the public.

That night I drove around inspecting businesses, which consisted of lighting up their business with a spotlight and checking for open doors or broken windows. As I drove to the westside of a complex called South Gate Shopping Center I saw two feet protruding from beneath a make shift cardboard shelter. It was raining and the shelter was inefficient because the person's feet were getting soaked. I realized that this individual was either intoxicated or deceased, because no one sleeps through such circumstances. The first thing that came to my mind was *"good deed."* I exited my vehicle in the rain and approached, after calling in my location. I pulled my PR-24 (night stick) and tapped on the bottom of his feet. He finally began to

37

stir, and I could smell the odor, which validated he was drunk and hadn't taken a bath in ages.

"What the hell, you want boy," he slurred? I had a feeling he had seen me through a hole in the box as I approached.

"Sir, are you ok," I replied? "There is a place just around the corner where you can stay for the night and get a hot cup of coffee and perhaps a sandwich and soup."

"I don't have any money for coffee," he shouted angrily. "Cops drink coffee and eat donuts, so do you got something on you?"

"I have some coffee in the car," I said, trying to maintain my cool. "Do you want the rest of it?"

"Hell yeah," he said. "Give it to me!"

As I began to get the cup of coffee I had just bought from the Circle K he yelled out, "Hey boy are you Black?"

"The last time I checked I was," I replied.

"They gave you a uniform and a gun," he belted out loud?

"Yeah they sure did and you know how dangerous that is," I responded, "a Black Man with a gun and in a police uniform."

"Are you planning on using it on me," he said as he stood up and staggered against the building trying to put his hands up in a boxing pose to protect himself?

"Not unless I have too," I stated as I put my hand on the handle of my pistol as a gesture.

"Well, I ain't going to no shelter," he said. "There are too many damn bums over there. You know you got to listen to a sermon before they feed ya?"

"No, I didn't know that," I quickly responded. "That's fine; you don't have to go there if you don't want to."

These words seemed to calm him down. He put his hands down and I set the coffee on the ground a few feet away from him and stepped back (Officer Safety). Just in case he tried to throw it on me. He took it and immediately began to drink as he leaned against the building. He then began to slide down the wall into a squatting position.

"You know in the eyes of God we are all brothers and sisters," I said.

"Ain't that a bitch, you and me brothers, unless you're calling me a sister," he retaliated?

"No, no, I am just saying whether we are male or female we are connected."

"I wonder what my mama and daddy would say if they found out," he said in a serious tone. "One thing for sure, one of them would have to leave the house. By the way, what the hell are you insinuating, that your daddy is my daddy or my daddy is your daddy," he responded looking confused?

I smile because I could tell he was serious. I saw my opportunity and I laid it on him about how God was looking out for him.

"Even my presence here tonight is an indication that God is smiling on you," I said. "You should examine yourself and see what it is that God has in store for you. I know its not sleeping out in the rain. You need to get up from this place and do something for yourself."

I could sense that I had his attention and he even stop drinking the coffee for while and just sit there looking up at me. He seemed astonished by my mini sermon and was speechless. I handed him half a sandwich and was really impress with myself. My pride began to swell as I walked towards my vehicle. Yes, I had witness for the Lord, gave food to transient and touched his soul. At least that's what I thought until I heard the coffee cup that he had thrown at me roll across the pavement. Then I heard his voice.

"Hey Nigger, are you out of your damn mind? What the hell are you talking about? There ain't no God, now get the hell outta here!"

I thought to myself, *I could go back and knock him out. I could also throw the cup back at him, after all no one would see me.* Then I heard a voice within my consciousness say, *"I would."* So I closed the car door, swallowed my pride and drove away.

Case 4: The Resurrection

One of my Sergeant's we shall call "D" for Desperate was a pretty good Sergeant with the exception of his egotistical narcissistic complex. To put it in simple terms, "D" was stuck on himself. He tried hard to show his machismo, which in reality was an attempt to conceal his insecurity.

"D" would go to the bars at night and wait for the drunks to come out and get in their cars. He would follow the vehicles until a violation occurred, then call his officers over to make a traffic stop and test them for Driving Under the Influence, and if necessary make an arrest. He called this proactive policing. I called it desperate and pathetic.

"D's" concept of policing was stats. He wanted his unit to have a high number of traffic stops, high number of DUI's, high number of misdemeanor arrest and high number of felony arrest if possible. He wanted stats even if he had to make it happen himself. To ensure these stats he would assign certain officers to areas around town where drugs were being sold. The only problem with this picture is that we were on patrol taking calls and we were not a special unit. The other units were angry because we were not taking our share of the calls and the call load was increasing. They certainly had the right to be irate.

One day, I responded to a check welfare call with another officer in the unit. The called involved an elderly lady. We found the lady had been strangled to death with a telephone cord. The suspect (s) had smoked a cigarette and drank a beer before they left the house. I thought *what arrogance and apathy?* The first person to respond to the scene to assist us was our Supervisor, "D." That's when I really saw his arrogance and self-centeredness. He had each of us to inspect his clothing to

39

make sure everything was perfect. We watched him comb his hair, wipe off his shoes, checked his breath and brush his mustache as he waited impatiently for the press to arrive. I was glad the press arrived so we could continue the gathering of evidence, and it got him out of our way for a while.

"D" was always looking for "stuff" and when he would check out at certain places we (officers in his unit) made sure we were as far away from him as possible. He would always call the officer that was closer to his vicinity to take the call, so we would check out as if we had something to do. If you were the unfortunate one to be called, by the time you arrived "D" would have the subject (s) seething in a high degree in pisstivity. It was as though he would tease a rattle snake and then hand him to you. Someone said it was like arriving at a hornets' nest after "D" had severely disturbed them, and he expected you to step in the mist and restore order.

We heard him check out early one morning on South Six Avenue and called in, "A man down, send paramedics." After a few minutes he radioed that the subject was DOA (Dead on Arrival) because there was no movement and the victim wasn't breathing. A few minutes later he requested that they cancel the request for paramedics and send Detectives and OME (Office of the Medical Examiner). After a few more minutes he cancelled the detectives and OME because the subject was breathing and conscious, but continue to send paramedics. After another minute he said cancelled paramedics because it appeared that the subject was only intoxicated, and he would volunteer to transport him to the Detoxification Center (LARK). Shortly afterwards he changed his mind again and stated he would not be transporting the subject to LARK, because the subject had walked away from him and appeared to be ok.

There was radio silence for about a minute and you knew the officers in the unit were laughing. Then Officer Bill added to the humiliation when he broke radio silence and he said, "May I please have the call number to **The Resurrection?**"

Case 5: Blood on the Shoe

While I was training a recruit we were about to end our shift when we passed by a hair salon and found what appeared to be a man sleeping on the ground. This is not unusual because in Tucson we have lots of transients, and we find them sleeping in the most peculiar places. Many times they are alcoholics and they pass out almost anywhere. Our climate is so hot that it seems to enhance the effects of the alcohol and it results in many alcoholics passing out in the streets, in someone's yard and there is no discrepancy as to where they drop.

We checked out on the radio and said we had a man down at a certain location. We parked and carefully walked over to the subject that wasn't moving. When we had gotten close enough to observe the person it was evident that he was dead. It appeared that he had been beaten to death. He had severe head trauma; his head was covered with blood and it had coagulated. There appeared to be shoe marks where he had been kicked and there were several rocks near the body that may have been used in the incident. After physically checking to see if the subject was dead, I told the recruit to stand still and turn and see if he could see his shoe tracks that led him to the deceased. We both were able to trace our tracks and we backed tracked in our own footsteps trying not to disturb the scene.

We called for detectives to respond and we taped off the crime scene and waited for them to arrive. After their arrival we assisted as much as possible but the case was now in their hands.

Later that day, we received a call reference a domestic violence at an apartment complex near the scene. When we arrived we observed it was between a teenage couple and friends of the couple. The young man had come home to his girlfriend's house and they were arguing about his whereabouts. He had been gone all night. He had apparently broken one of the statutes of domestic violence and we were in the process of physically arresting him. When we talked to the female she mentioned that he had been out all night and when he came over to the house he had blood on his tennis shoes. When she asked him about the blood he became belligerent and an argument occurred.

Since we had just recently been involved in a case where the man was beaten to death and probably kicked, the light came on. We advised detectives and they proceeded from there. We later learned the suspect in the domestic violence and his friends had beaten to death the person found at the hair salon. He had admitted that the blood on his shoe was probably that of the victim. He was arrested for a homicide. I thought it was rather unintelligent for him to walk around with tennis shoes that had the victim's blood on it, but it was even more pathetic to get in an argument and invite the police into your home while you still had on the shoes.

Case 6: Rabbit in the Bush
I had grown up in the Rillito/Marana, Arizona area and we hunted rabbits, quail, doves, javalina and anything that was edible. When you're hunting in the dessert you learn to observe all things, especially part of the environment that seems odd. You get a sense about nature and you become very sentient to your surroundings. Something that doesn't belong to the area or is not endemic is easy to spot.

We were looking for a transient who had committed a larceny (theft) and had run to the dessert area near by. When I got there the officers who had responded initially said they had checked and couldn't find him. I decided to give it a go and exited my vehicle where his last visible tracks were detected. I could see his tracks going into the high grass. I returned to my vehicle and drove around the small grassy area looking for tracks that would show the suspect had came out of the area. I could see no tracks where the suspect had came out so I returned to the point of the last tracks and walked in the grass tracking each step. I walked about fifty yards into the high grass when I saw what appeared to be a cavity in the grass ahead. I was apprehensive of walking upon this guy without a warning, so I drew my weapon

41

and prepared to get the guy to stand up by bluffing him in thinking that I knew he was there.

"Hey buddy," I said in a calm voice, "if you're willing to stay there all day I'm not. If you want to get up slowly showing me your hands I won't shoot." I waited for a moment listening to him stir in the grass. "Honestly, I probably wouldn't shoot you any way," I said, trying to get him to think about his options. "The items you stole aren't worth it."

I could see he was there, because the grass started moving even more than before. I didn't know if he had a weapon or if he was on his stomach or back. If he were on his back he would be able to see me if I approached from a certain angle, but if he was on his stomach that would limit his vision.

"Well, good buddy, I tell you what I'm gonna do!" I shouted. "I'm gonna get on the radio and call for a dog unit." I had already called in for backup and the officer that was initially there was responding.

I yelled, "You're probably an ole country boy, so you know how temperamental those dogs are. They go right to you and start biting and gnawing away. The sad thing is they bite the part that stink the most and that will probably be your butt or your groin area, and that includes your penis, because you probably haven't showered like you should!"

I had no knowledge about the police dogs at that time, but what I said made sense to someone else who didn't know. It was then I got a response.

"How many dogs you think they're gonna bring," he shouted?

"I don't know, probably five or six, why," I replied almost laughing? "You figure on giving up?"

"Yes sah!" he replied.

"It don't matter how many dogs they send," I retorted, "you know you can't fight even one if you're lying down."

"Hell Nah! I ain't gonna get ate up by no dogs," he shouted as he stood up with his hands elevated towards the sky.

"Damn you're good," he said. "You've got to be a country boy? Hell the first guy that came out damn near stepped on me."

I made him continue to face away from me and put his hands on his head. I approached him from behind and cuffed him and I could see he had covered himself with the long blades of the grass, because the grass was stuck in his clothing. My backup had arrived and had parked nearby the edge of the grass and was walking towards us.

"Is there anybody else out here," the Officer shouted?

"No," I said. "He said he does have a partner that lives about a mile away in the desert in one of the camps, but he wasn't involved."

The transient was an elderly White male, very thin and pitiful looking. He explained that he had eaten a meal and skipped out without paying.

"And for that, I damn near got ate up by dogs!" he bellowed.

"Dogs, what dogs are he talking about," said the officer? "Hell is he crazy. They're not sending a dog out here for someone who skipped paying for a meal."

"I was just flattering him," I replied. "Sometimes people just need to think they're worth something."

"Hey, he's right! I was kinda flattered that they would send dogs out just for me," he said. His back was to me and as he turned he responded, "Damn, you're Black, too." He appeared shocked that I was a Black Officer.

"Since the day I was born," I replied. "A couple of times in my life I wanted to change, but I got over it."

"It would be an honor if you would let me ride to jail in your car, Mista Policeman," he said.

"I think I can arrange that sir," I told him.

"How did you find me," he asked? "What made you come out and look for me when the others had left?"

"It was like looking for a rabbit in the bush," I replied, "you just didn't blend in and the bent grass left an unusual gap."

I transported him to the restaurant where he had eaten his meal and the waiter identified him as the suspect. He did have a local address and no warrants, so I cited and released him. I made him think that I was doing him a favor.

I saw him from time to time in the desert, and he supplied me with information about what was going on in the area. He knew the specific prostitutes that would come out to the desert with their johns and who was involved in drugs and so on. I never had another problem concerning him, and I made several arrest based on his information.

Case 7: Church Folk: Missionary

When you are both a Police Officer and a Christian you feel that if I work with criminals on my job and having to deal with bad attitudes and anti social behavior, perhaps when I'm off work I can take a break. This is not so when you are a minister and some of the leaders of the church are no different from the criminals you deal with while on duty. Bad leadership is bad leadership no matter whether you are in, or out of the church. There are criminals in and out of the house of worship.

It seemed that God allowed me to be under siege and bondage the first few years of my Christian life. Many of us would come to the church with a headache and a little money, and leave with a bigger headache and broke. When I look back on the conditions I went through in the church, I can't help but think of the Israelites in Egypt and the journey through the wilderness. I often referred to these times as my wilderness journey.

There was an alleged missionary in the church that was everything but a missionary. When you are a Police Officer you can detect certain things and when

God calls you, you have a certain ability to discern. There was something about this woman that was not just right, but I kept it to myself.

One day the Pastor presented to the church a situation.

"Well," he said, "our missionary have been arrested and falsely accused."

We sat patiently as he rendered his opinion based on what she had said. Being an officer I could detect there was some inconsistencies with her story.

"She was in her motel room while at a church convention and the police broke into her room for no reason and arrested her; they probably broke into the wrong room by mistake," he stated. "She called and needed the church to bail her out and she would pay them when she got back home."

I knew that police officers didn't go around breaking into people's rooms for no reason at all. Even if it was a mistake there was still a reason. You had to have a warrant or exigent/urgent circumstances. If it was a mistake, why did they arrest her? There were just too many unanswered questions.

The churches that had us under bondage never had any money because the Pastor took it all, so he was asking the members for an offering to send to her. Most of the time when things would come up and the Pastors would ask for money, I noticed that they never gave any themselves. There was no such thing as a treasury, because the church was always broke.

When I was first called to the ministry God spoke to me and said, "Watch the preacher." I thought I was going to see all these virtuous acts that would be seared into my memory to help the people, but instead it was just the opposite. I know now that God was preparing me to be a pastor and was allowing me to see all the things that I shouldn't do. I saw the epitome of deception, greed and egotism in the church among them so call, leaders.

While the others were responding out of their ignorance, I thought, *I am a police officer and you can't go into someone's room without a warrant unless you're in hot pursuit of a felon and they run into the room with you behind them.*

I held on to my money and investigated this further by calling the Phoenix Police Department and talking to the officer working the case. He responded by saying our so-called Missionary had been under surveillance when they noticed several men coming and going from her room. They stopped the guys and were informed that she was prostituting out of her room. She was known by their Vice Squad and had done this on other occasions. They had gotten a search warrant and she was busted. I never told the Pastor this because I believed he knew the truth from the beginning. Without my help she was back at church the next week.

The following week I received a call while on patrol that a member at a certain church had been asked to leave and she was outside the building throwing rocks at the windows. The Pastor wanted her arrested for criminal damage and disorderly conduct.

When I arrived and talked to the Pastor of this particular church, who was also a friend, I was informed that it was her, our so-called missionary.

"She was using all kind of profanity," he said, "it was so bad I dare to repeat what she said."

"Sir I need you to tell me what she said," I stated.

He would not say what she said, as if he would be punished if he repeated the curse words that she had used. "I don't think God would mind if you quoted her so I can determined if there was a threat or not."

"Sorry preacher," he said, "I just can't get my mouth to say those words."

I conceded to writing that she used profanity, was disruptive during the service and threw rocks at the window. She was fortunate that she didn't break anything or it could have been a felony charge for damage to a church.

After a brief search I found her, all two hundred and fifty pounds trying to hide in a phone booth like she was superman. I approached the booth and knock on the folding door with my baton.

"Minister Colter is that you," she said while squatting on the floor of the booth?

"Yes maam," I replied, "and just what are you doing changing your disguise?"

"I was just about to make a phone call," she replied.

"And just how do you do that," I interrupted, "squatting down with the phone still on the hook?"

"Oh," she said, "I guess I lied?"

"Yes maam," was my response, "I guess you did. What happened at the church this morning?"

"Ain't nothing happened!" she belted. "Those no good heathens need to get saved!"

"Well," I snapped, "from talking to the people it appeared that you were the one acting like a no good heathen?"

She then feigned crying until I told her, "Sorry, that's not going to work honey, I know what's real and what isn't."

She regained her composure quickly and admitted to being disruptive and then going outside and throwing rocks at the glass windows.

"Why would you do something like that," I enquired?

"Cause I was mad," she blurted out, "plus I was just doing what the Lord told me to do."

I looked her over for a second and starred into her lying eyes. "You mean to tell me that the Lord told you to go to the church and raise hell during the service, then get mad at the people and go outside and throw rocks at the windows?"

"I'm telling you, Preacher. The Lord works in mysterious ways," she said aloud so passer byes could hear her. She seemed to know that she had center stage.

"Oh I agree with that," I replied, "so consider this ticket God's doing."

She was relieved that I wasn't physically going to take her to jail. I would not have written her a ticket, but the Pastor insisted that he wanted to press charges against her for her actions. She was one of those situations when the only way to get the message across is to arrest them or cite them.

Three days later I was working the evening shift when I received a call to respond to a disturbance at a trailer park. When I arrived at the location I walked to the door of the trailer in questioned and knocked. I wasn't surprised when the door opened and the so-called Missionary was standing there in an open robe with nothing under it. As she revealed her private property to me she pretended the belt to her robe accidentally came loose. I think she was hoping for someone else.

"Why don't you close your robe," I insisted. "You could either catch a cold, or customer, and since I'm not a customer, it would probably be a cold."

"Hi Preacher, you been following me around," she said hopingly with a smile.

"Actually I guess I am," I said, "because my job is to seek out crime and criminals and when I do that I keep running into you."

"I ain't no criminal, am I," she blurted out inquisitively?

"I don't know, you tell me. We received a phone call informing us there was a disturbance here and when I knock on the door you come out half naked? It seems that I have seen more of you than is necessary."

"That phone call! Oh that was my boyfriend," she whispered as she loosely tied the cloth belt around her robe leaving her breast yet exposed, "but he's gone now. He got mad and left."

"Can I look around and be sure you didn't kill him and make sure you're not trying to hide his body," I responded sarcastically?

"Preacher," she said laughing, "you know I wouldn't do nothing like that. Come on in and see. Ain't nobody here now but me."

I looked carefully and found no one. Apparently the alleged suspect had left or she just wanted some attention and hoped a male officer would respond.

"Is this over with," I asked, "or is he coming back?"

"No he done left me here all alone," she said as she began to slowly undo her robe. "I got something to ask you," she said. "Look at me!" and she twirled around like a model. "Look at my body. I'm still a young woman. Don't you think it's all right for me to have a man, because I still have needs?"

I knew this was an attempt to seduce me, but a two hundred and fifty pound woman was a bit much to be trying to model and she definitely wasn't tempting. It was like watching an overweight Shinaynay on the Martin Lawrence show.

"Close your robe and I'll tell you," I said. "Is the man you're talking about your husband?"

"Nah, it's my boyfriend," she said in a whisper as she took her time about closing her robe. Again leaving her breast exposed intentionally.

"Well, is your boyfriend somebody else's husband," I asked?

"Hell no!" she then corrected herself, "I mean, heavens no!"

"Look, you are either involved in fornication or adultery," I said, "and neither one of them is right. The scripture says *if we look upon another person with lust in our hearts then we have sinned.* I think you have gone further than looking."

"Yeah," she said, "but women are different than men…"

I interrupted, "but sin is sin, I don't care which gender is committing it. The Word says to, *"Flee fornication; every sin that a man doeth is without the body; but he that committeth fornication sinneth against his own body"* **(1Corinthians 6:18, KJV).** I could tell she didn't have a clue about what I was saying, probably because she never read the bible.

"Will you pray for me that I find me a man," she retorted in a voice feigned with sadness?"

"No, I will not!" I nearly shouted, "The man is suppose to find you, not you find him."

"Ain't you a preacher? Ain't you suppose to pray for people if they have a problem or a need," she shouted?

"Yes I am," I replied, "but praying for you to get a man is not the answer to your problem, in fact, I would be creating a problem for some man."

She gave me a look that was empty of understanding, so I tried to make it simpler, "if you are having problems with men, then getting another man doesn't solve your problem. What you need to do is examine the behavior that is causing you the problem in the first place."

"Yes, but, but!" she bellowed as I started for the door to let myself out.

I could see that her conversation was intended to keep me there and she had no intent of resolving her problem in any other way other than being with a man. I advised her to take up the matter with her Pastor because I could only tell her the truth and that wasn't what she wanted to hear. I already had her information from previous run-ins and I told her to have a nice day and left.

The following Sunday we visited another church and there she was testifying to the honor and glory of God about how saved she was and how she was living a life without sin. The people stood to their feet and gave God the praise, because He had given her the strength to live a sinless life.

Well, not all of the people stood up. My wife and I sat in our seats and watched the show. She was pretty convincing if I didn't already have the scoop. In fact, she looked me right in the eyes when she testified, "I'm saved and sanctified, Holy Ghost filled and fire baptized, and I thank the Lord for Jesus in my life."

As I looked at her that day I thought about the words of the Lord when he said, *"A good tree cannot bring forth evil fruit; neither can a corrupt tree bring forth good fruit. Every tree that bringeth not forth good fruit is hewn down, and cast into the fire. Wherefore by their fruits ye shall know them. Not every one that saith unto me, Lord, Lord, shall enter into the kingdom of heaven; but he that doeth the will of my Father which is in heaven"* **(Matthew 7:18-19, KJV).**

I felt pity for her at that moment because I knew if she didn't change she would be one of those trees hewn down and cast into the fire.

I had taken my wife to another church in a futile attempt to escape bad leadership and a few weeks later the Pastor was asking for money as always. He said there was a need in the church and they had to get five hundred dollars. I was amazed at the nickel and dime psychology that was used to try and get money from the people.

My sister told me once, that the most pathetic person is a fool who thinks he is a genius or an idiot who thinks he is intelligent. I saw this scenario play out many times on Sunday morning, "fools pretending to be geniuses and idiots thinking they are intelligent."

Many days I would be in the church witnessing these antics and saying to myself, if I really wanted to make some arrests, all I had to do is go to different churches and listen to some of these Pastors for a few minutes and then arrest them. Most of them could be charged with fraud, extortion, and theft or embezzling.

The Pastor's brilliant plan to get five hundred dollars was simple.

"I figured out a plan how we can get the five hundred dollars," he said. "The Colter family (which was me) can pay two hundred and fifty dollars and another family which he named could pay the other half. Now ain't that a good plan," he bellowed, proud of his ingenious solution to the problem.

The astonishing thing about this was that the congregation stood to their feet and applauded. It was a very short applause because the other Lady and I stood up and in a very articulate and subtle way we told him, "You must be out of your cotton picking mind."

We sat down and since he was so ignorant he was still trying to figure out if we had agreed or disagreed with his proposal. Immediately, the so-called missionary, whom I had arrested several times stood up and told the Pastor and the congregation that she would pay the whole amount.

"I will write you a check for the amount," she said. "Ya'll don't have to worry about a thing."

Again the people applauded. She had made commitments like these while visiting other churches and she never gave them a dime. I noticed before the end of the service she pretended to go to the rest room and slipped out the door when no one was looking. I think it was for the better, because we never saw her again, either in the church or on the street.

She is probably in prison somewhere running a revival. Like she said, "God works in mysterious ways."

Case 8: Church folk: Preacher

I often did taxes after work and tried to help many of the church folk. I found that they were the worst about lying on their tax returns. There was a certain preacher that had about as many problems and issues as a sea has waves. After sitting with him for what seemed like hours I was able to get back all his withholdings except ten dollars. He was so frustrated that he couldn't get back every dime he tried to intimidate me in writing down his dog as a dependent and claiming his children twice. When I advised him that he would have to answer to the IRS if he was audited he got angry. I left him and his "tax return" in the house and went home.

I was later informed by a friend that worked at H & R Block that he had came in and asked them to do his return. When they finished he was getting back his withholding, with the exception of two hundred dollars. He became so belligerent that they had to call the police. He crabbed a chair and threw it through the glass window and ran from the establishment. You must understand this is a minister or shall I say church folk. If he would have listened to me he would have gotten it all except ten dollars.

This same person later came to the church and threatened to attack family members. On one occasion the Pastor had all the men to get in a circle and hold hands as we prayed. While praying outside the door of the church the subject took matches from his pocket and would strike them and throw them at us as we prayed. We continued praying for the situation and asking God to deliver us from his antics. I don't know about the rest of the guys that were in the circle, but a college friend and I prayed with one eye open. I didn't trust this guy and if he would have made the wrong move the prayer meeting would have been over. My friend and I would have thrown him to the ground and hog-tied him until the police arrived.

On one other occasion he went home (the preacher) and put a gun up to his wife's head and pulled the trigger a couple of times. God would not allow the gun to shoot, so in his efforts to see if the gun was working he pointed it towards the ceiling of the house and pulled the trigger again. This time the gun fired. If it weren't for her praying and believing in God her life would have been over. You must understand I'm talking about church folks.

Chapter VI
Mirasol Task Force: Introduction

I worked on a task force that was trying to cleanup South Park and surrounding areas. We were fighting everyday against drugs, crime and the poor living conditions that faced the community. We had the option to arrest or get the people help through various resources. The Urban League, Food Bank and some Rehab Centers worked with us and made it possible for us to help many, rather than throwing them in jail.

Sometimes during cold weather we would contact the Urban League, and they would help the resident to get their electricity turned on or supply them with food baskets if needed. The Director, Mr. Clark, was a very distinguish African American who seemed to care. He provided us with the use of his counselors and what other resources that was within his power.

My partner was a young officer who I shall call Ted and he was a dark skin Mexican. Some of the people in the neighborhood thought he was African American. We were assigned for the purpose of eradicating criminal behavior and drugs in this certain area. The police also needed someone to work in the area so they could get to know the people. Ted had the personality to fit and he was a good officer in spite of what others may have said. Ted was very dark skinned and we passed him off as a brother. Many times the guys in the hood would refer to him as the other brother with the good hair. The girls saw him as an attractive guy, and I think that may have been the source of some of his problems. I must admit that all the years of my life I have never seen a guy that looked handsome to me. He was a lot younger than me and his energy level was sky high.

Ted was an excellent officer and a dear friend, and I loved him as a brother. Sometimes I felt like tying him to a tree and whipping him with a belt to beat the spirit of infidelity out of him. He had the normal common police problems: pride, women, infidelity, drinking and gambling.

He wasn't racist like some who worked the area and each of us saw each person as an individual. If any one tells you that they are not prejudice and that they see everyone as the same color, get away from them because you are listening to a liar. If they say whenever they look at a person all they see is a man, they don't see if he is Black or White, please run from this person as well, because he is a liar and he is not very smart. People are not the same color. All Blacks are not the same color nor are all Mexicans the same color and sometimes society makes a difference in color even within the same race. There are so many identifiers you must look for when you interact with people. It doesn't make us any less important than the next person, but it does make us distinct from one another.

As a police officer, the first things you better notice is that person's race, age, gender, their economical situation, know their culture and be aware of cultural biases and know their education level and so on.

It bothers me when a person looks at me and don't see me. They see me as Black man, but they don't see the rest of me. That is called stereotyping. All African Americans are not the same, all Mexican Americans are not the same; all Asian American are not the same and all Caucasians are not the same. People must be treated as individuals, but the above factors are to be considered in order to have effective interaction and communication.

We never denigrated the people in the streets and we treated everyone as human beings. The problem was trying to get the people in the street to treat each other like human beings. Many people thought Ted was my brother, others just thought he was a brother who could speak Spanish. He would often tell them he was a brother with straight hair. Ted's biggest problem was his private life. Many officers' career interfered with their private life, but with Ted, his private life interfered with his career. He did have some problems and they concerned women. He was always having wife and girlfriend problem. That's normal when you try to have both.

There is an old Negro spiritual that says:

I told you once, and I told you twice
You can't get to heaven
With a sweat heart and a wife

I tried to encourage him the best I could, but I still had to tell him the truth. One particular girl he was dating had a "fatal attraction attitude" and would follow us around. We would be on a call and she would be in her car on the other side of the street watching us. I would also talk to him about his drinking, but he would justify himself and say he deserves to have a good time. His idea of a good time was spending his money with some woman other than his wife and drinking himself into oblivion. I continued to peck away at the mountains in his life but he kept building them up again.

Our Sergeant and I picked cantaloupes together in Blythe California our senior year in high school, and we had played against each other in sports. It seemed that somewhere along his career he got on someone's bad side and people who didn't know him were always trying to put him down. To be honest with you, I think his problem was being White and having too many friends that were minorities. Perhaps he just wanted to do the right thing, and treat everyone fair. He did lean towards minorities and had a special place in his heart for anyone with a need. He was well respected in the Black and Mexican communities and that didn't set well with some commanders. Even the bad guys respected him. He would talk to the young, old, preachers, drug users, drug addicts, it didn't matter they were all God's children. If they were right, they were right and if they were wrong, they were wrong, and he let them know it.

He was meticulous and apprehensive about things and because of these peculiarities the officers made fun of him. Before every raid he would make sure that everyone had his or her shoelaces tied with a double knot. Apparently during a raid in the past he must have tripped over his shoe laces and never forgot about it. He would have me to pray before we left and would double check and triple check everything. I never thought it was anything wrong with him being extra careful, especially when dealing with human life. I truly felt that without him I would have never been able to receive my Master of Counseling Degree. He was very helpful by putting his officers first. If it hadn't been for my Sergeant being the person he was Ted would have gotten into more trouble than he did. He told me in secret that if I ever felt being with Ted was an officer safety problem let him know. Though there were times we would be followed by Ted's girlfriends and were spied on by them, I never told the Sergeant.

The Sergeant went over and above his duty, but if God had been his Commander he would have laid up many treasures in heaven to await him at the end of this earthly journey.

He made sure that we took people to detoxify or counseling, got food for those that needed it or connected them to the Urban League and other resources. If we had to, we arrested them. Believe it or not some people just needed arresting.

I think one of the saddest things about being a Black Police Officer in Tucson is you knew there was no consolidation among Blacks. Those that had rank could care less about the other Black officers. They even seem apprehensive about talking to you in public. When you went into their office and talked about an issue, they whispered as if they were afraid someone would hear. They would close their doors and pretended it was for confidentiality, but in reality they didn't want their fellow White commanders to see them talking to another Black Officer. They would pretend to be your brother until a White commander came around then everything suddenly got formal. Their anxiety with you in their presence was perceptible.

Let's be honest, the White commanders took care of White officers and those they liked. The Mexican strictly took care of Mexican Officers, and the Blacks well they hid behind the issue of being politically correct. If you needed help, the last person you should go to would be a Black Person with rank. We (Black Officers) didn't ask for anything out of line, just to be treated fair and just. Judge me by the content of my heart, my ability and desire to work hard, and if I fail, at least I had the opportunity. But don't disregard me for fear that you might be seen as someone that helped his own. I found that all my breaks came from commanders of other races rather than African American.

It is disappointing to know that slavery still exist. Emancipation Proclamation took the Blacks out of the plantation, but it did not take the plantation out of the Blacks. The slave owners learn that to keep slaves in check, they had to turn us against each other. They made a difference in color, gender, looks and etc. Then they applied status according to those differences. Whatever it took to cause us to fight among ourselves, that is what they advocated. They then learned that if you want to hold a slave in check, put another slave with an attitude over them. That concept still works. If you want to keep Black workers in check, put a Black male or female over them (A Black female preferably because they pose little threat to the White social order). The next best thing is to get a Black male that wants to be White. Then, there is the male or female that is involved in an interracial marriage, and is afraid he will "rock the boat." Malcolm said that "good people come in all colors," well, so do bad ones.

One day Ted came to work sad and looking as if he had lost someone he loved. Actually he was very close to doing that. He told me that his mother was in the hospital and the doctors didn't know what was wrong with her. If they didn't find something out he could lose her. Immediately I had him to take me to the hospital. When we arrive his mother was very weak and the sickness had taken its toll. I had him stand next to her and take her hand. I laid hands on her and began to pray until God's anointing fell in the place. I knew when I left there that God had stepped in. Ted had tears in his eyes, but I told him every thing would be all right. The next day his mother recovered and the doctors let her go home. When Ted told me about her healing I knew that he himself had realized that God was still in the healing business. The doctors couldn't explain what had happen, but Ted and I knew and so did his mother.

I didn't know if the word had gotten out, but another officer came and told me his wife had cancer. He was very distraught and asked me to pray for her. I told him that I taught a bible class and would bring the class over and pray for her in his home. He invited us to come over and we did. We laid hands on her and prayed that God would move her cancer and heal her of her disease. I advised him that the doctors can fix things, but only God can heal. I am glad to say that God healed her of her cancer and they went on to have a family.

Case 1: Prejudice

One day while working in the community with another officer that I will call "Tee" we saw prejudice first hand. Tee and I went to a house in the Vistas and there in the yard was a junk vehicle. All of the statutes applied to this vehicle to make it a junk vehicle. The vehicle was in a yard surrounded by a fence and there was no gate big enough to drive the vehicle out. It was like the "ship in a bottle." We left a sticker on the vehicle and made contact with the owner. He stated he was a Jew and declared right off that he hated Blacks. We left and when we returned after a number of days the vehicle was still in place. We followed the procedure for progressive enforcement and gave him a few more days.

When he refused to adhere to any of the rules and totally disregarded the law we decided to give him a civil citation. His wife was very understanding, but he called us every name in the book or shall I say out of the book.

"You guys can't help yourself," he shouted as Tee was writing the citation. "Both of you are nothing more than field niggers and your parents are the same." He continued, "That's what's wrong with the Department, there are too many of your kind working and polluting the neighborhoods. I know important people in this city and you guys won't have a job much longer. Then you can go back to Africa where you belong."

"That's great," I stated, "I wish I knew a lot of important people."

He continued to denigrate us as he followed us to our car. After I got in the car I complimented Tee for his temperance.

"I wanted to knock him out right there," said Tee, "but I was too busy recording everything he said."

"I wished you would have told me!" I said. "I was shocked that he had a recorder in his shirt pocket and had turned it on.

"I remember dealing with him before," he said, "and this time I was ready for him."

A few days later we went to court and the Magistrate was an African American that I had known since childhood. We started talking and he started talking about the bible. He took his bible out of his desk and showed it to me.

"Without this (referring to the word) I am nothing," he said. "There is no way I can have a job like this without God providing it."

When Tee showed up he was also shocked that the Magistrate was Black. The biggest surprise of all was when the complainant came in and saw three African Americans sitting around the table waiting for him. The Magistrate decided to give him another chance and said we were to report to him in a certain number of days. If the complainant didn't comply the citation would stand.

When the days expired we face our Jewish friend in court again and this time he was cited. He decided to appeal the case stating that we were all prejudice and he was treated unfairly.

Months later we faced him again in a higher court and this time the judge was Caucasian. After hearing the facts and listening to the tape that Tee had submitted for evidence the judge became livid with the defendant and handed down a decision. The citation stood and the court ordered the complainant to do community service work at an African American Organization.

Case 2: That's My Sweater

It seems that in certain parts of every town there are a few houses that are notorious for problems. Well, Tucson is no different. There was this one house that always had something going on that was outside the law. One of the guys who were always into drugs had brought his wife down and was renting the house. They were living there, but the drugs and the criminal activity never ceased. For their sakes we will call them Tommy and Dee. We got to know Tommy good because we were always running him on the computer almost every night. It never failed that he would have a warrant or was a suspect in some burglary or robbery. We talked to Dee and she seemed like a decent person. I could never figure out why some women are determined to hook up with people like Tommy. He was headed nowhere and had nothing to show for the years that he had lived. He always tried to be more intellectual than he was and it showed, because you can't hide ignorance and stupidity very well if you talk too much.

Dee on the other hand had an education and had some college. She was a nurse and made honest money, but Tommy kept spending the money and getting in trouble until finally she lost her job. He would show up at her job and cause a disturbance, until the place of work could not take it any longer and she was let go. He would steal from her and sale whatever she didn't tie down.

Ted and I had a little talk with both of them and Tommy "went off," telling us how dumb we were and how we were oppressing the Black man. He said he was too smart to get caught by us because we were too dumb.

"Ya'll too dumb to catch me doing anything," he boasted.

A few days later we had a robbery at one of the convenience stores and the store camera took a picture of the suspect. When Ted and I saw the photograph we knew it was Tommy. This guy had his face partially covered and he had on a girl's sweater, but we could tell by the physical features that it was Tommy. It wasn't enough so we took the Sergeant to Tommy's house and told him to show the picture to Dee. We never told her anything about the picture we just showed it to her.

I call her over and said, "Hey, Dee take a look at this."

Her first response was, "that's my sweater! What the hell is Tommy doing with my sweater on? He told me he didn't have it then he goes out and take a damn picture with it on him. I wondered what had happened to it!"

She had no idea she was looking at a robbery photo of her husband in action. We did all we could to keep from laughing aloud. She was so upset about the sweater that when we told her it was a robbery photo, she continued picking out things on the photo to identify Tommy.

When we arrested him, I reminded him that he had allowed two dumb cops to catch him. I had told him in the past, "Just keep on doing what you're doing and eventually you will get caught."

I asked him, "If we are two dump policeman and we caught a criminal, then how dumb was the criminal that got caught?"

I realize that people without God cannot change. The liar will continue to lie, the thief will continue to steal and the robber will continue to rob. Tommy had gone beyond the counseling or the verbal reprimand. He had three strikes against him and he never tried to take advantage of any of our offers to go to counseling or get help from other sources. He was sent to prison for armed robbery.

It seemed that every day we made arrests or we got someone to volunteer to go to detox or counseling. Many times when the offense was minor instead of arresting them we would give them a choice. There were those that were determined to try, and they would go and get their house in order so they could leave for a few weeks or a month to rehab. We would make the arrangements and they would show up at a certain location to be picked up. Some made it and some didn't, but the few that did make it, made it worthwhile to us to continue helping.

Being a police officer can be an eye opening experience. Many times I would see so call church folk, out in the streets, at the crack houses or doing something they had no business. It ranged from pastors, to ministers to missionaries, to deacons and regular members. Our children as well are being drawn to the streets, because Satan's hold on this world is strong. We must continue the fight for our children and loved ones.

Case 3: Fish Out Of Water

One night I saw a familiar face and Ted stopped the patrol car to investigate. It was one of the members from a neighborhood church. He was hanging out with the users on the corner trying to score some drugs. It was Charlie (name changed) who just a few weeks ago had joined the church. I think Pastors are so caught up in getting members that they don't ask if they are saved or not. Unsaved members or new converts should receive teaching and guidance to help them to be stronger in their faith. Unless you give your life to Christ it doesn't matter how many churches you join. Having a lot of members isn't the purpose, but getting souls saved is.

There was an old deacon in our church that we all called, "Papa." We had just gotten a few new members and I had gone to Papa's to visit. When I told him about the new members he seemed sad. When I asked him why he was so sad, he said, "Son, mo people mo devils!"

When Ted and I approached the crowd they dispersed. There was Charles and he was in so much pain he couldn't run. He said he had just gotten out of the hospital after being operated on one of his internal organs. I was sympathetic with him but I said, "Charlie I know why you're out here and you have no business being here. You look like a fish out of water."

Charles was like many folk. He was like a caterpillar that kept crawling in and out of the church. I told the saints at our church "only God can change a caterpillar into a butterfly."

I stated, "I know you're out here messing with the rock (crack cocaine) so don't try to lie to me."

He initially denied it, but the circumstance, including the time of night and his environment took away any alibi.

"Yeah, you're right Rev" (they called me Rev. or preacher man), said Charlie.

"Charlie," I shouted, "you can't be in church on Sunday and out looking for crack on Sunday night."

"I know, I know," he said, "I'm going to leave here right now Rev and go home and tomorrow I'm going to church."

While Charlie was talking a strange feeling came over me and I began to prophesy to him.

"Charles," I said, "God is telling me something about you and you had better listen. If you don't get off these streets and return to him, you will soon die on these streets. You had better make your choice tonight because time is running out."

"Tomorrow Rev," he said trying to sound convincing, "tomorrow I'm going to give it to the Lord, because you're right, there's nothing out here for me but trouble and death."

He spoke with urgency but his words were full of vanity. It was convenient words to use to get away from the heat that was on him. I embraced him and as I walked away I shook my head in doubt because I knew unless Charles got off those streets something drastic would happen. God had told it to me and when God speaks you better listen.

Ted and I was a two man unit working the night shift a few days later when we got a call of a man down at our favorite spot. We responded code three (lights and siren) to the location. When we arrive others were there scanning the area. Ted dropped me off with the victim and continued driving to locate the suspect who may still be in the area.

One good thing about this Department is, with the exception of a few officers (they know who they are), we will respond immediately to any area in the city without hesitation or prejudice. If you need a medic unit they will be there A.S.A.P., and it doesn't matter what part of the city you're calling from.

I exited the vehicle and realized there was a man on the ground just a few feet from the house. Paramedics were there on the spot and were trying to treat him at the scene. I assisted them and realized at one point that the person on the ground was Charles. His breathing was labored and it seemed that each breath was his last. They did the necessary preparation at the scene then transported him to the hospital. The blood poured from his wound and next to him was a wine bottle broken with alcohol dripping from the broken glass. They took him away and I knew I would never see Chares alive again. Prophesy was about to come true.

There was a female standing on the sidewalk crying and identified herself as Puddin (name change). I tried to calm her down and when she recognized me she did calm down somewhat.

"He's in the house," she said. "He's in the house!"

"Who's in the house," I replied?

"JP," she shouted, "he's the one that did it!"

"Did what," I asked wanting her to talk about the situation?

"Him and Charles were fighting and wrestling on the ground and Charles was on top of JP. JP got up and Charles was running behind him, he stopped and came back to where I was standing; we started walking and he just fell to the ground and didn't get up."

She took a deep breath and continued, "This all happened over a damn bicycle."

I advised the other officers that JP was inside of the house and after talking to Puddin I had gotten a mental picture of what had happened.

Ted and I went into the house and there was JP sitting there nervously wringing out his hands. Another officer had come into the house before us and was asking JP questions. He wouldn't answer the questions and you could see this was something that had come upon him unexpectedly. He had that hopeless look and a look of disbelief that this couldn't be happening to him. JP had already done some time for attempted murder and appeared nervous. I approached him knowing he wasn't going to say anything to the White officers.

"Are you ok JP," I asked, concerned about him and his state of mind. Immediately he recognized me and started talking. I really wanted to advise him of his rights, but I hadn't asked him anything about the incident. I just said, are you ok?

Officers know that if a person volunteers information the best thing to do is let them talk.

"Colt," (short for Colter) he said. "He started this! Charlie started this. He has had an attitude towards me since High School. I was here minding my own business. I was cutting up some chicken for dinner when Charles and Puddin came over here asking about a bicycle. I don't know why she brought Charles over here because we have never gotten along. I told them to take the bike but Charles started talking shit. I told him to just leave, and then the Nigger started throwing rocks at the house and at me. I had my butcher knife in my hand from cutting the chicken and ran out into the yard and again told him to leave. He had a wine bottle and came toward me in the yard. I was standing on the sidewalk in front of the house when he approached. He threw something at me then grabbed me and we started wrestling."

I just let him talk. I was writing down what he was saying and so were the other officers. They gave me a signal to keep him talking. I gave JP a non-verbal sign by shaking my head back and forth as if I was showing disappointment in Charlie's action. As JP was talking I could see that in comparison Charles was almost twice his size.

He continued, "He grabbed me and we fell to the ground and he was on top of me. I had actually forgotten that I had the knife in my hand. He was hitting me and I just started pushing upward with the knife. I managed to get away from him and run to the house. He was chasing after me cursing and threatening me. Next thing I knew he was walking away with Puddin and he passed out on the sidewalk."

Apparently Charles was so drunk that he didn't realize he had been stabbed.

Puddin said she didn't realize JP had stabbed Charles with a knife. She said he had turned away from arguing and chasing JP and was walking with her a few feet before he collapsed to the ground. Charles died on the way to the hospital that night.

JP was advised of his rights and repeated his story to the other officers. He told them he had thrown the knife in the backyard and later we were able to retrieve it. JP was tried but was not convicted. After talking to other witnesses it was determined that Charles had provoked the incident. It was also apparent that Charles had an ongoing thing with JP and was always perpetrating trouble between the two of them. If only Charles would have taken heed to my warning, he may have been alive today. I guess he realized perhaps on the way to the hospital in a moment of consciousness that when God speaks, you had better listen.

Case 4: "Crack" Case

Mirasol Park Area was considered the little crack center of Tucson. It seemed that all the small time drug dealers started out from Mirasol Park and then branched out from there. The novice drug dealer began at Mirasol, which was located in the South Park Area. There were very few houses in the area that didn't have someone associated with drugs in some way. Whenever you drove down the street in a police car you could hear whistling like a canary and see lights flashing, if it was at night. They were all warning each other. They even had a radio with our frequency. We knew that certain families could hear us when we switched over to our so call private line where officers could talk to each other without interfering with the main frequency.

We would play games with them, and as Ted would say we, "pissed them off." Sometimes we would get separate cars and talk to each other as if we were about to do a raid on a certain street. We knew they were listening and since they didn't know which house on the street we were going to raid it posed a problem for them. Normally they would transfer their dope to a different house or if they had to they would flush it down the toilet. Ted and I would mock a raid.

"You ready," he would say?

"Wait until the others line up," I would respond. "We have so many cars involved we have to get our timing right."

"The only way they're going to get rid of the drugs is they will have to flush them down the toilet," Ted hinted, "We have enough search teams to find anything they hide. This time we're going to search the yards, the toys, the little baby's diapers and everything."

This gave them something to think about. We both gave the sign and turn on our siren and lights. He came from the west end and I came from the east. The players were already at their doors or standing by their fences to see if we were really coming. The street was sounding like the bird cages at the zoo with people whistling, blowing whistles and the toilets flushing probably brought the water level down a couple of feet.

We would pull up to each house and stop and as soon as they would close their doors we would go to the next house. By the time we finished it only took about a couple of minutes, every player on the street was pissed off to the highest degree of pisstivity, because they must have flushed pounds of drugs down the toilet except those die-hard users that needed their stomachs pumped out afterward.

The next day we would visit the players on the streets and they would tell us how they out smarted us because they knew we were coming.

"Damn," Ted said as he kicked the ground in feigned frustration, "ya'll outsmart us again. That's why we called it off; I knew you guys were a step ahead all the time. The other cars didn't even come because they had gotten word that you guys knew we were coming, but next time it will be different."

"Damn! Damn!" Echoed Ted as we walk to our cars, "I told you Colt these guys are on to us." He said it loud enough that they could hear and they immediately started mocking us.

When we entered the vehicle Ted had to drive fast to get us out of there so they wouldn't see us laughing.

Case 5: Wanna

We had some disappointing days working with the addicts. There was a certain girl, "Wanna" (name changed) that had several children and was pregnant with another. We were determined to help her, but any food or clothing we gave her she traded it for drugs. We would get food from the food bank or the Urban League and she would turn it into drugs. The Director would provide us with food, clothes, counselors or whatever was needed. He always tried to help. He would make arrangements to have light bills paid and rent or whatever was within his power to do. He tried to help those in the community to help themselves.

We had gotten all kinds of food for Wanna so she could eat healthy because of the baby she was carrying. No matter what we did she would always be out on the streets trying to get dope. I knew she had several warrants and we were waiting for the opportune time to arrest her. We saw her driving a car, knowing she had suspended license and a warrant. I couldn't believe she could be as bold as to drive by us and wave. We pulled her over for a minor traffic violation and could see in plain view paraphernalia. I had her to step out of the car and asked if she had any weapons. She handed me her purse to check after she took out a tissue. She pretended to wipe her face with the tissue then dropped it on the ground. Ted knew what was going on and immediately picked up the tissue.

"I know you don't want us to arrest you for littering too," he said.

"Hell Nah! Give it back to me and I'll throw it in the trash," she said nervously reaching for the tissue.

"You all right," said Ted mockingly? "Damn girl you sure are nervous over a little piece of tissue."

We knew there was something in the tissue that made Wanna nervous.

"What the hell is it that got you so tense over a snot rag," belted Ted?

"I know what it is Ted," I said. "There is a secret message written on the tissue."

"Ain't no damn messages on that tissue fool," she said angrily. "Why ya'll make such a fuss over tissue paper is beyond me."

"You're not going to believe this;" I said sarcastically, "some of the real dumb drug addicts will wrap their drugs in tissue paper. I know you wouldn't do something like that, but believe me the real dumb ones will."

She had this shocked look on her face as if she may fall into that category. Ted slowly unfolded the tissue, as a stripper would slowly take off her clothes. Wanna stood there in anticipation ready to defend herself, if and when Ted would reveal his findings.

"I don't know why you're doing that," I said to interrupt the suspense and referring to his mode of unfolding the tissue.

Ted stopped for a moment and then resumed slowly unfolding the napkin. I said in her defense, "You know Wanna ain't that stupid as to put drugs in that tissue."

"I know that," said Ted. "I know Wanna isn't that stupid, I'm just checking to clear up things for Wanna."

Wanna was about to urinate on herself, because she knew there was drugs in the tissue and Ted was taking all day just to unwrap it. Wanna couldn't handle the suspense of Ted slowly unfolding the tissue, so she blurted out, "Hell just take me to jail; I don't have time for this shit. If I have to stand here and wait for him to unwrap that damn tissue like he's peeling an onion, I'd rather be in jail watching a soap opera."

"Jesus Ted," I said, "the girl does have a point. Are you going to unwrap that tissue or not?"

Ted stood in front of Wanna and unwrap the final folds of the tissue. There were five pieces of crack pressed within the tissue.

"Ooowee," said Wanna as her eyes fastened on each piece of crack. "Who the hell put that crack in that tissue paper?"

"I don't have a clue," I said, "but isn't that the dumbest and stupidest thing you ever saw?"

"I know who did it," said Ted. "It was the invisible man. I wished I could see him I would kick his ass and arrest him for possession."

"Me too," replied Wanna, "I'd kick his butt myself."

"Ted," I said, "watch your language. He could be a good person. Maybe he was trying to hide it from Wanna and wrapped it in the tissue paper."

"Ain't no damn invisible man, ya'll crazy," she said, "Hell take me to jail so I can get away from all three of ya'll."

"Wanna there are only two of us," responded Ted, "the invisible man isn't on the Force."

"Yeah he is," she said half smiling, "you and the Preacher, and that damn invisible man who put the crack in the napkin can all go to hell. Take me to jail so I can get away from the three of you."

We took Wanna to jail, but they wouldn't accept her because she had abscess sores from doing heroin and needed to go to the hospital first. We took her to the hospital, and they treated her for the abscesses. They had to give her a shot right into the abscess and she was hysterical.

"Wanna," I said curiously, "what's your problem? You take shots every day when you're taking drugs."

"Hell, that don't mean I like em!" she screamed.

"Would you prefer that I hold your hand or something?" I said this kidding, but Wanna was serious.

"If you don't hold my hand," she cried, "I ain't taking no damn shot!" So I held her hand. Then she said, "Ain't you a preacher?"

"Yes I am," I replied curiously, "you know that why?"

"Can't you pray for me or something," she said with her eyes now overflowing with tears. Her demeanor started to change and she wanted support for what she was going through.

"Yeah, I'll pray for you if that's what you want," I said trying to settle her down.

"Now, shit I'm scared," she shouted. "Tell God to help me now!"

"Well, I think he heard you, but I'll pray anyway," so I prayed in a low whisper in an attempt to get her to quiet down.

"Shit, you got pray louder so he can hear you," she belted! "Hell I can barely hear you myself!"

I elevated my voice and prayed louder so God could hear me better, just for Wanna. So there I was, holding Wanna's hand praying for her because she was an addict afraid of needles. Her belly was stuck out like she was about to have a baby at any moment and there she was crying with her face buried against my shoulder. We were probably a sight to see and some of the staff was certainly looking at us. They were probably wondering if I would pray or not. When I finished praying and closed my prayer by saying, amen. Wanna also, said amen, and I also heard several amens coming from the staff.

At that tender moment I realized that she was still one of God's children. She was nothing less than a lost sheep. She was about to become a mother again and was probably someone's sister or daughter herself. She was indeed a precious stone in God's jewelry case, rough and unrefined but yet she belonged to God. It is written: **"behold all souls are mine; as the soul of the father, so also the son of the son is mine; the soul that sinneth; it shall die" (Ezekiel 18:4, KJV).**

A few days later she had her baby and it was born deformed. I don't know the details but I am told it may have died due to the lack of prenatal care it didn't receive while she carried it. There were some rumors that the baby may not have died, but she gave it away. I would ask Wanna from time to time about the children, but she would only respond, "They're fine" and walk away trying to avoid a conversation. I think because she allowed me to see a side that was forbidden it bothered her. No one wants to allow themselves to be transparent to just anyone.

One day Ted advised me that he knew where she was living. We went by her apartment and took inventory on what we thought she needed. We went to Mr. Clark at the Urban League and secured several food baskets and took them to her. I heard on the streets that much of the food was sold for crack.

I saw Wanna scarcely after that day. She moved or just dropped out of sight and we couldn't find her. We never saw her on the streets any more. I had heard that she had gotten off the streets and off drugs.

Years later, my daughter was visiting a friend. The friend's mom had to go to work so the next-door neighbor volunteered to bring my daughter home. When my daughter came home she told me the lady that had brought her home said she knew me from a few years ago. I went to the car leery of whom she may be and that she knew where I lived, thanks to my daughter.

I approached the vehicle and saw a nice looking lady getting out. I knew the face was familiar but I couldn't remember her. She walked up to me and embraced me. She wrapped her arms around me and buried her face against my shoulder and said, "thank you." She then returned to her vehicle and drove away with tears softly finding their way down her cheeks and onto her dress.

As I stood there my daughter said, "see dad, I told you she knew you!" I slowly turned to my daughter and said, "I don't have a clue who she is, do you?"

She said, "Yes dad, her name is Wanna."

Case 6: Dead Baby 1

The most overwhelming thing for me as an officer was to see injured or dead children. While working in the South Park Area in the 80's and 90's there were deplorable situations in which people had to live. Tucson is a city that has warm weather almost all year, but there are a few days in some years where the temperature drops unseasonably low. Sometimes in the winter the temperature would drop to the point of freezing during the night. I unfortunately had to respond to a trailer where a baby was not breathing. When I arrived medics were already there trying to revive the child. I talked to the mother who seemed rather calm over the situation. She said the baby had a slight cold and some how rolled over face down in his pillow. The baby being too weak from the cold or flu couldn't move himself to breath. We checked the trailer and it was freezing inside, which didn't help the situation at all. The temperature on the inside was no different from the temperature on the outside. The baby was blue when we found him. Medics transported him to the hospital where he was pronounced D.O.A. (dead on arrival).

I watched as the doctors tried to resuscitate the child. I thought about my children when they were that age and my heart melted with pity. At the hospital they had opened the baby's chest to massage the heart, but it was too late. I stood there alone in the room after everyone had left. I thought about how precious are children to the Lord. It is written: ***They brought unto him little children that he should put his hands on them, and pray: and the disciples rebuked them. But***

Jesus said, Suffer little children, and forbid them not, to come unto me: for of such is the kingdom of heaven" (KJV, Matthew 19:13-14).

I thought of the many lives that had been cutoff by the untimely death of this child. If he had lived, perhaps one day there would have been a wife and children, maybe even grandchildren. How many lives would he have touched? How much greatness died with this child? Who died in that trailer that day, a doctor, lawyer, perhaps a great athlete, or maybe a president? I thought of the innocence and the humbleness of a child and how Christ used children as examples to get his message across. The Apostle Paul said, *"Be ye therefore followers of God, as dear children"* (KJV, Ephesians 5:1).

The father came in and he was devastated. He took the baby that was wrapped in a sheet and covered it with kisses. He cried vehemently as he held it close to him. He gazed upon his son with great pity. I was reminded of the scriptures, *"Children's children are the crown of old men; and the glory of children are their fathers"* (KJV, Proverbs 17:6). Psalms 103:13 says, *"Like as a father pitieth his children, so the Lord pitieth them that fear him."*

I touched his shoulder and told him I was sorry for his lost and if he needed me I would be outside. I went outside to get some air and saw the mother sitting smoking a cigarette. I went to her thinking perhaps I could say something that would comfort her.

"Your husband is inside with the baby would you like me to take you inside," I said quietly.

"Hell no!" she belted. "What the hell for?"

"Don't you want to see the baby before they take him away," I whispered, "perhaps you may want to hold him?"

"Hell No!" she blurted out again, "Why should I want to hold a dead baby?"

"That dead baby is your son," I said trying not to show my contempt for her response. "If you don't want to see the baby I think you should at least comfort your husband. He is taking this rather hard."

She looked into my eyes and I saw no remorse whatsoever.

"Hell no!" she said and walked away.

Apostle Paul talked of the relationship of the older women to the younger: *"That they may teach the young women to be sober, to love their husbands, to love their children"* (KJV, Titus 2:4). Maybe this was her way of dealing with her lost, but it appeared that she had no love for her child and a burden had been lifted from her shoulders. The child's death was ruled as natural causes, but I wonder if she gave nature a little help, or did she refuse to give any help at all?

That day the trailer was marked as a crime sight. During the investigation we discovered there was no heat in the trailer nor was it fit to live in. It was later condemned and removed from the area. It was too bad that a child had to die to get someone's attention.

Case 7: P.C.P.

Ted and I had dealt with all different types of drugs that came through the neighborhood. It appeared that crack cocaine was the most destructive on a short-term basis. We also had encounters with Angel Dust or PCP. Part of the composition of this drug is embalming fluid. PCP was known as the "superman drug" because it made people feel like superman. They would have super strength and had been known to jump out of three story windows and not get hurt. It also had other side effects: those on PCP were always taking off their clothes and they didn't like light or heat because it irritated their skin. If you ever came across a naked person, you almost knew if he wasn't exposing himself and it appeared that he was oblivious of his nakedness, he was on PCP.

I received a call one day and Ted was in a separate vehicle but he came as my backup. Our arrivals were synchronized and we exited our vehicles about the same time. There on the porch of one of the motel rooms was a young Mexican Nationalist male. As we got closer to him we could see he was sitting in a chair apparently waiting for us. When he stood up to greet us it was obvious that he was naked. Ted and I both looked at each other and our thoughts became one.

"Ah shit!" blurted Ed. "It's gotta be PCP! Let's just be cool," he said in a low voice, "I don't think he can speak English so I'll do the talking."

I called for an ambulance because usually paramedics didn't have the proper restraints that were necessary.

We introduced ourselves to him and pretended not to notice that he was naked. I don't think he knew he was either. The subject could not speak English and was from Mexico. We convinced him that we only wanted to check his pulse, but in order to do that he would have to lay on the gurney with the straps. Ted told him that he would have to strap his arms just for a little while so they could get a good pulse then we would unloose him. Amazingly he went along with everything until we tried to strap his feet. Then he realized what was happening and the fight was on. His whole body was wet with perspiration and he kept slipping out of our grasp. The most disgusting thing was since I was the biggest; I had to lay across his legs with his penis stabbing me in the side. Ted thought this was funny but I beg to differ.

We finally got him strapped down and to the hospital and while waiting in the room with him he began to lose it. He started flexing his muscles and it appeared the straps were going to come apart. He was lying on his back but he rose up and down so fast that the stretcher started moving across the floor of the hospital room. We were afraid he would tilt the bed enough to fall over. The doctors came in and we had to keep him stationary enough so they could give him a shot to settle him down. This guy was about five feet, two inches tall and weighed about one hundred and thirty pounds, but he had the strength of five men.

After about two hours he started coming down from the affects of the drugs. I thank God that he allowed us to put him in restraints before he realized our true intentions. Why anyone would allow himself or herself to be controlled by such a drug is beyond me. I don't think the victim even remembers the trip. Some of them are not fortunate enough to come out of it alive.

I realized that God had protected us all in this situation. I remember the words of the psalmist that said, ***"The Lord is my rock and my fortress and my deliverer; My God, my strength, in whom I will trust; my shield and the horn of my salvation, my stronghold. I will call upon the Lord, who is worthy to be praised; so shall I be saved from my enemies"*** **(Psalms 18:2-3, KJV).**

This guy had better be glad he had two officers with a conscience, because it could have been someone who would have started out beating him with a PR24 (Night stick) or drawing down on him with a gun and hoping he made the wrong move. Were there officers like that on the Department? Well, you be the judge, what do you think?

Case 8: Dead Baby 2

I again responded to a trailer located near the projects in reference to a possible D.O.A. When I arrived I knocked and was let in by a Black female. She had on excessive clothing and after walking into the trailer I could tell why. It was colder in the trailer than it was outside.

"Did you call the police," I asked?

"Yeah, I think my baby died last night," she said trembling from the cold. "When I checked him this morning he was cold and kind of stiff."

"Where is the baby so I can see him," I asked. I did a quick visual of the trailer as I followed her directions to the baby? She led me to a certain part of the trailer and hesitated about going any farther.

"He's over there in the baby crib," she said as she pointed in the direction of a small bed surrounded by rags.

I walked slowly in the direction of the child scrutinizing the surroundings. When I saw the child it was obvious that he had been deceased for a while. There was mucous covering his nose and his eyes were mattered shut. A single thin blanket surprisingly covered him. His mother was clothed with a sweater and a jacket, but she covered her baby with a thin blanket.

I called for the proper units to respond and waited for the investigators. I talked to the mother because I had responded to the trailer in the past due to drugs. She said she had been there all night. When you are a police officer you have a sense about people and I felt that was a lie. I went back inside to look around and when I came out she was gone. When she returned I confronted her about leaving, suggesting that she had probably left the baby during the night as well.

"What can be so important that you just had to leave," I said? "Never mind, I know. Only drugs can make you leave your dead baby here and disappear."

"No, I went to call my mother and let her know what's going on," she replied defensively.

"That sounds good, but I know for a fact that your mother is not around," I said.

"Oh, did I say my mother? I mean my friend," she said attempting to correct her lie.

"One thing I know Rosie," I said, "a lie can not stand alone. If you tell one lie you have to tell another to support it. Now tell me, how many lies are you going to tell to support the first lie?"

"Ok, I had to do something. Is that better?" She replied.

"Did it have to do with drugs or would you rather not say," I questioned?

"I'd rather not say!" she retorted.

"That means it had something to do with drugs," I belted!

I got in her face and as I reprimanded her she started crying. It was then that I realized she was only about fourteen or fifteen years old. She was a baby with a baby and had no idea about taking care of a child.

Office of the Medical Examiner (O.M.E.) was called due to it being an infant child. They said due to congestion and because he was sick with a cold or flu he stop breathing.

I don't know why the mother would not have had the baby under close scrutiny if she knew he was ill? That is what happens when Children have children and there isn't any support or guidance. They are totally void of parental skills and knowledge on how to raise a child. As a child she probably wrapped up her doll the same way. There were no charges of neglect or abuse against the mother.

Again the questions arise: What great thing could this child have accomplished? What was his destiny or his potential in life? What was the fate he escaped? These were the questions that a dead baby couldn't answer, but they spoke to my heart every time I saw a dead child.

Case 9: The Penis is a fake

I was patrolling Mirasol Park and I had scared away a few potential drug deals. It was pretty obvious because the cars that came into the neighborhood stood out like a bright shining star. It was evident that certain expensive make cars didn't belong to the area. The dealers would stand on the corner and when they saw me they would beckon the vehicles to continue and not stop. I would just park where the activity was and in plain view and eventually they would spot me and leave and go somewhere else.

It's amazing to me how people that are doing wrong always draw so much attention to themselves. College kids on their break would take a taxi to the neighborhood to buy drugs and they always took the taxi company whose drivers knew where to go to get drugs. This was because most of the drivers for this particular company were doing drugs themselves.

On this one occasion a van came into the neighborhood and parked near the Park waiting for a dealer to service him. He could not see my vehicle but all the dealers could. They beckon him several times to move on, but apparently he didn't get the message. I figured this is a person determined to score or someone new to the area and not familiar with the signals. Finally I drove from my position towards him and when he saw me he drove away. Like I said, those involved seemed to draw attention to themselves. His registration was with another state and expired; his brake lights weren't working; the vehicle sounded like an army tank because it had no muffler, the turn signals didn't work and he did nothing manually to compensate when he made a turn. I allowed him to get out of the neighborhood before I stopped him and radioed for Ted to take my spot at the Park.

I followed the subject out of the neighborhood, but I didn't have to stop him, he stopped himself when he ran out of gas. I parked behind him with my lights flashing and slowly walked to the driver's side of the vehicle. I asked him for his vehicle paper work and advised him that I followed him from an area where signs were posted "high drug activity area." I could tell when he spoke he had a New York accent.

"I know why you were there," I said. "Didn't you notice they were telling you that a cop was around the corner?"

"Yes sir," he replied. "But I don't use drugs. I was there looking for a friend."

"What's your friend's name," I asked. "Perhaps I know him?"

"Ah ah, damn I forgot," he replied, sounding almost as stupid as he looked.

It was at this point I realized he had a marijuana joint stuck over his left ear. I maintain my composure and kept from laughing.

"You know marijuana will do that to you," I said. "It will make you forget things. So you don't do drugs," I stated while looking at the marijuana cigarette planted on his ear? "What's in the back of your van? Is it ok if I look?"

"Hell yeah, go right ahead Officer, like I said I'm clean." He was still unaware of the soulrette (marijuana joint) resting on his ear.

He opened the back door of the van after wrestling with the door for a couple of minutes and overcoming all the niches involved. The first thing that caught my attention was a dildo about a foot long. This was not something a man would carry around in the back of his vehicle.

"This yours," I said? "Maybe it wasn't drugs you were looking for."

"Ah damn, you're not going to believe this, but that is not mine," he said, seemingly embarrassed. "That belongs to a couple that had my van last night."

"I certainly hope not," I replied. "I never knew you could detach it and lay it around when you're not using it. Maybe I should try that and put it back on at night when I get home."

He actually blushed and got embarrassed. I glanced at his license that he had given me and it was a New York license.

"New York!" I said aloud.

He responded, "Yeah New York. I know, I know, it's a long way from home."

"New York," I called him, "that's a long way to drive for some drugs and a fake penis."

"No Officer Colter," he said after gazing at my nametag on my uniform shirt. "The penis isn't mine."

"New York, we have a very serious problem here," I replied. "If this penis isn't yours and I know it isn't mine, then we have someone walking around this town without a penis."

I could tell he was still high on something. Maybe it was the marijuana he had been smoking or the crack. He thought he was enlightening me when he blurted out, "Officer that's not a real penis!"

"It isn't," I responded sarcastically. "I'm glad you straightened me out. I was about to get on my radio and ask for everyone to be on the lookout for a man without a penis."

I continued looking through the debris near the back of the van. "What else is back here," I asked?

While I was scanning for the obvious there next to the dildo was a glass crack pipe with one end burnt and the screen still inside.

"This is paraphernalia, you know," I said as I stuck my pen inside the glass tube and placed it carefully in an envelope I had on my clipboard.

"You know I can dust this for prints and I'm sure yours will be on it," I stated, hoping to eliminate another lie.

"Please officer!" he begged. "I'm just trying to get to a friend's house who said he would help me to get out of town. I'm trying to get back to New York and I pray that I still have a job," he pleaded.

"You're out here in Tucson smoking crack and weed, you have another man's penis in your van and you have the audacity to pray that you still have a job in New York," I replied almost angered by his remark. "What do you really know about praying?"

"I know that's the only way I'm going to get my life back, by praying to God to get me out of this town," he cried.

"Why did you come here in the first place New York," I asked?

"Man, you might not know this," he said, now crying, "but Marijuana and other drugs are cheaper here. I thought I could score some and go back home. Well I scored but I haven't been able to get back because I started using it myself. I have a good job in New York and I work for a radio station."

"Are you Big Time in New York," I asked?

"I guess you could say that, but right now I'm nothing," he whimpered as he continued crying.

"Everybody is somebody in the eyes of God New York," I said. "One thing I've learned in my walk with God. You never look down on a man unless you're picking him up."

"Are you a minister or something," he said, as the tears begin to flow even more frequent?

"Yes I am," I said, "and right now I think I'm the answer to your prayer."

"Officer, I know this is out of line," he said, "but could you pray for me?"

"Not until you do me one big favor," I replied.

"What's that?" He asked, as he wiped his eyes with his shirtsleeve.

"Would you give me that marijuana joint that's stuck behind your left ear first," I said pointing to his ear.

"Damn," he said, and then he immediately apologized. "Excuse my language sir, but I didn't know I had that up there. I guess I forgot. If I had remembered it was there, I would not have come to the park, at least not until later."

"Well," I said, "I heard the mind is the first to go and then the rest of your body. God works in mysterious ways," I said. "Maybe this is one of them. Now let's pray."

I prayed for New York that day. Then we both agreed if he would destroy the dildo and throw the remains away in the dessert, I would not charge him for the crack pipe and the marijuana joint. I will do what we call a long form, and I will put it in evidence as found property and give you a chance to get out of town. We both did what we said. I then pushed him and his van to the nearest gas station and gave him my last five dollars that I had for lunch. He put the five dollars of gas in the van and added a few cents more.

"New York," I stated, "I'm going to take a chance on you, but if I ever see you around here again you can give your soul to the Lord, but your butt is mine."

He shook my hand and promised me he was headed out of town.

"I'm going to pay you back," he said. "The next time you see me you will know that I am telling the truth about cleaning up and I believe I'm going to get my job back. I got a friend that said he would give me traveling money, and I'm out of here."

New York then drove away and as I waved I prayed within myself, ***"Lord let it be your will and deliver him and draw him nigh unto thee."*** I knew I would never see him again if he were serious and if he wasn't he would not get a second chance.

A year later we had put up more signs around the park making it a "No Drug Zone." The celebration at the Recreation Center culminated with prominent people speaking out against drugs. The press was there and there were people that were dressed very dignified standing around. Our local government officials, the Chief of Police and members of other agencies were all present.

There was a distinguished young gentleman who starred at me during the ceremonies. I did not want to talk to him because I never like talking to the press. They have a way of turning things around. One thing I learned is that when someone from the press says, "this is off the record," you better stop talking. There is no such thing as "off the record."

I was able to escape him for a moment and when I looked for him, he had disappeared. I returned to the room and there he was, right in front of me. He came up to me and started to reach in his pocket. I tactfully put my hand on my weapon just in case.

"Are you Officer Colter," he replied?

"Yes sir, I am," I said. "Can I help you sir?"

"You already have," he said, he had tears forming in his eyes, and as he wiped away his tears with his shirtsleeve. He opened the wallet he retrieved from his pocket and took some money out. It was a new five-dollar bill.

"You don't remember me do you? I owe you this," he said. "I want to thank you for giving me a chance and believing in me."

"I'm sorry," I said, "but I don't know you."

"You probably would remember if I showed you my penis," he said with a smile, "but you made me cut it up and bury it in the desert."

"New York!" I said aloud, "Is that you? I didn't recognize you at all."

"All the way from the Big Apple itself," he said. "I guess I clean up pretty good. I took some of the dirt off and put on some clean clothes on the outside, but thank God I'm clean on the inside as well."

"Man you look good," I said, still marveling at the difference in his appearance from the last time I had seen him.

"I told you I had a big time job in New York broadcasting on the radio," he said. "I said when I get it together I would repay you for what you did. I took a flight from New York to thank you and my other friend for helping me and I'm going back this evening. I heard about this little celebration and I prayed you would be here."

He put his arm around my shoulder and said, "You have no idea of the number of people you're saving off these streets just by being understanding and praying with them in the midnight hours."

"I do try to rescue them, but only God has the power to save them," I replied. "I'm just trying to get them to open the doors of their hearts and give him permission to walk in."

"Well, it worked for me and Christ is now my Savior," he said, as his voice faded away due to emotions and he cleared his throat. "I just want to say thank you and don't ever stop doing what you're doing. God has made this your purpose."

He shook my hand and pulled me close to him and gave me a hug and walked away saying, "I got to catch a plane."

As I stood there Ted came over to me and asked,

"Who was that?"

"Just a friend," I said, "a brother in the Spirit."

Case 10: Corky

There was a couple that I had known since I was young. He and his wife were very influential in their younger days and were involved in the NAACP. They attended the church that my mother-in-law had attended before she died of cancer. They were just parents trying to raise their children and did the best they could, but it seemed that all the teaching of morals, ethics and values sometimes goes in one ear and out the other.

I guess Corky (name changed) was one of those people. He had an excellent job but some how his wife got hooked on crack and disserted him and the kids. Corky in his attempt to follow her around and get her back got hooked himself. His mother and father were taking care of their kids while they were out destroying themselves through their drug habit.

Corky's wife seemed to be a total mismatch for Corky. I don't know why people seemed to be attracted to opposites. Corky was the type of person that if he cleaned up he would look decent. He was very articulate, but for some reason he loved this woman. It was a morbid attachment because he was willing to become like her just to be with her. He was willing to leave his children for this woman.

His wife on the other hand seemed to be the type of person that all the water and soap in the world couldn't make her look any better. She was indeed a person that only God could clean up from the inside out. It was denigrating for him to be out in the streets, but he was there running around with other crack heads and chasing his woman. His mother had told me that he was out there and if I saw him let him know that the kids loved him and they wished he would come home.

Every time I would see him in a crowd I would yell his name out loud. The crowd would disperse quickly and he would disappear. One night Ted and I saw a group in front of the After Hours Nightclub. The club was closed and there they were just hanging out on the corner chipping off whatever piece of crack they could get *(Chipping is a term used when a user scores for someone else and they chip off the rock as their payment for their service).* They lived for that little piece that the buyer would break off for him. But in most cases he chipped it off for himself before he gave it to the buyer.

In Tucson you could buy: a Black man's rock or a White man's rock. The Black man's rock was almost twice as big as the White man's rock. Perhaps because the Black man would buy it and chip off it before the White man got it. He couldn't do that with the brothers because they knew better and they knew the true size of a twenty-dollar rock.

This night I was able to grab Corky while we let the others get away. The first thing he said to me was, "Officer Colter why are you doing this to me?"

"What am I doing to you Corky," I asked? "This is the first time I was able to catch up with you."

"You're always calling my name and nobody wants me hanging around them," he answered, "and they think I must have done some great crime for you to be looking for me personally."

"Well, you have," I said. "You have committed one of the biggest crimes of the century. You have disserted your children."

"I love my kids, Officer Colter, but this stuff is something else. It's demonic and I know it, but I can't stop!" he shouted, as if he was partially apologizing. "I pray about it then I go right out and get more."

"Where is your wife, Corky," I asked?

"Man I don't know and I'm starting not to care," he cried. "Chasing after her is what got me out here in the first place."

"Chasing after her is only an excuse, but it was still your choice to use it," I said, trying to remind him not to point fingers.

"Man all I know is I wanted my wife back. I left my kids for her and this (referring to the crack pipe in his hand). That's a damn shame!" he shouted. "Can't nobody help me but God, and He stopped listening to me long time ago."

"Maybe the reason He stop listening is because you aren't serious," I replied.

"I don't think those who have never smoked crack can even begin to realize the power it has over you," he cried out. "You think you can handle it, but you can't." Corky continued, "This ain't about physical or psychological addition. There is something else to it; I think this shit gets in your spirit and its evil."

"Now you're making sense," I said. "There is a spirit behind it brother and the only way to fight spirit is with Spirit. The word tells us, ***"For the weapons of our warfare are not carnal, but mighty through God to the pulling down of strong holds"*** (2 Corinthians 10:4, KJV). **The bible tells us that,** *"we wrestle not against flesh and blood, but against principalities, against powers, against rulers of darkness of this world, against spiritual wickedness in high places"* **(Ephesians 6:12, KJV).**

I said to him, "God's Spirit is greater than any spirit on this earth, but without Him you're in trouble."

"What weapons do we have?" He replied.

"Prayer for one," I said.

"Pray?" He blurted out. "I told you I did that and nothing happened?"

"Corky," I said, "it's about the condition of your heart when you say it. You have to mean what you say. God knows you can't get off crack by yourself. No one can. If God don't give you the strength it can't be done. But to get that strength, you have to believe in what you say and truly want what you ask for."

"Officer Colter," he said, "do you know that there are people out here that actually pray that God will allow them to score some drugs?"

"Yeah and you're probably one of them," I replied.

"You know they call this crack pipe, the devil's di-k," he said, "and I'm tired of sucking on it. I'm tired of running. I'm tired of doing drugs; I'm tired of living like this. Look at me. I look like a bum," he said holding his arms up in disgust. "I haven't bathed or brushed my teeth in I don't know how long. When you're out here the first thing that goes is hygiene. You don't give a damn about nothing but crack." Again he lifted his hands up in the air frustrated and asked, "How did I get this far?"

He started crying and leaned against the wall of the building. "God, what have I done," he said as he hit the wall with his fist.

"All I know Corky is you don't belong out here. None of you do," I said. "You're searching for deliverance in all the wrong places and you can't find it in drugs. The biggest problem is you can't find the answer because you don't know what to look for. What you want isn't what you need and you certainly can not fill a spiritual void with a natural thing."

"I know what I'm looking for, a way to get through each day," he replied, "just like everyone else out here."

"Drugs may get you through today, my man," I answered, "but it guarantees that you will be back the next day with the same problem or worse."

"How do I get out of this mess," he uttered?

"Brother there has got to be someone or something in your life more important than drugs," I said, trying to get him to think about his children. "Begin to focus on those things."

"I think about my parents and go right out and do drugs, he replied. "I think about my children and still do drugs."

"You got to have both the inspiration and the power and you can only get that through Christ. That's your only way out of this hell," I said. "You better make up your mind soon or you will die thinking about it."

"Man, I got to stop doing this shit, its killing me," he said while trying to wipe away the tears.

"Maybe this is a part of the journey you have to go through to find your purpose," I replied.

"What is my purpose Officer Colter?"

"I don't know Corky, but I do know what your responsibility is, and one of them is to take care of your own children." I continued, "I know you need to be the son that your parents raised you to be. I know that the only way you're going to accomplish any of that is you first have to go through God to get there. He is the only avenue you can take to get your answer."

I had totally forgotten about Ted who had walked away and was standing next to the car. Every once in a while he would take out his handkerchief and wipe his eyes, but never said a word.

I took the pipe from his open hand and continued talking to him. "The first thing you need to do is to get off these streets, but before we take you to a shelter or home you need to pray with a sincere heart."

Corky had covered his face in his opened hands. He was crying aloud, "Lord please help me!" I put my hand on his shoulder and we both began to pray a sinner's prayer, then we asked God for deliverance and for strength and faith. That night God begin a work in his life. We took him to detox and called his parents. When he reached the Detox Center, his brother was working that shift and registered him.

Two weeks had passed and we hadn't seen Corky. I hoped he had made it. The following week we had a neighborhood meeting at the Mirasol Center and Corky's parents were there. His mother came up to me and said he was home and back to work. He had gotten his old job back and was taking one day at a time. She embraced me and said, thanks for what you did for my son. She too had tears in her eyes and her husband was just as appreciative.

Satan is taking our children away, and if we are serious as parents, we should be willing to go to the depths of hell to get them back. Tell that Devil these are my children; in the name of Jesus take your hands off of my children.

Case 11: That's Some Nasty Stuff

Ted and I would go to Mirasol Park and see several players hanging around a certain area. As we would approach, they would walk away. We had gotten smart to their tricks so when they walked to the other side of the park to get away from us we would scrutinize the area where they had hung out or the place they had recently walked away from.

They would put their drugs inside the trashcan in a plastic bag or wrapped in tissue. Often they would put it under a trashcan and wrap it in foil or wrap. They would also dig holes in the ground put their crack inside the hole and cover it with grass or debris, but it was obvious because the ground would appear to be freshly disturbed. Sometimes they would hide their drugs and paraphernalia under rocks or in holes in the trees or in the crevices between branches. We knew almost all the hiding places and when they would see us discover their drugs they would kick the ground in frustration and give us the finger. We could tell whom the drugs belonged to by who reacted to our discovery. On many occasions the dealers were so hard up that they would not trust anyone so they kept their drugs on them.

On one occasion I chased a dealer/user around the corner and apprehended her. She took out a bag of marijuana and started eating it. I thought this would be interesting so I let her go ahead. I watched as she ate about a third of a bag of marijuana. She became so frustrated because the bulky substance had become a challenge. She stopped after a while because she was choking and spit out what was in her mouth.

"Damn, that's some nasty stuff," she said coughing and gagging.

"I thought you were enjoying it," I responded. "I was curious and wondered if you would eat the whole bag."

"You were going to stand there and watch me choke," she shouted in frustration?

"Nah girl," I replied, "I would have slapped you on the back. I was just curious to see if you could really do it. I thought you would at least take it out of the plastic bag first."

She handed me the bag of marijuana that was left and then extended both arms for me to put on the handcuffs and replied, "Shit, take me to jail this shit is making me sick."

"You have anything else," I replied, "Let me know now because when I search you and find more I'm gonna ask that you it eat."

"Hell nah!" she said, as she lifted her dress up and pulled down her panties. "Look, do you see any drugs?" She was standing there nude and showing all of her business to the whole world, and the officers that were close by.

"Why did you do that," I asked, disgusted with her? "You just gave these guys the answer to all the questions they have asked about you. Now, they all know what you look like naked because you don't respect yourself."

"Damn, you're right, just look at them," she said showing some embarrassment for what she had done. The officers that were watching started salivating at the sight of her naked body being presented to them at no charge.

"Girl you ought to be ashamed," I belted as I got in her face. "Pull up your panties and put down your dress. Just because you're Black you don't have act like that. You might think it's cute, but everyone that is starring at you thinks you are a fool."

"Look, I'm sorry!" She belted. "I don't even know why I did that."

"I know and I believe you know too," I said, implying that she was high on drugs.

"No you don't! You don't know why I did it either," she shouted, fishing for an answer.

"Girl, look at you!" I replied. "You're hanging out at South Park where the drugs are. You have been smoking and eating marijuana and I don't know what else. You are always hanging out on the street with half naked hookers and you have the audacity to tell me that you don't know why you're acting a fool by revealing your naked butt to everyone on this block?"

Lina dropped her head for a moment and when she lifted her face I could see the tears begin to form. Slowly the tears dropped one by one, and then the embarrassment of what she had done flooded her soul.

"I ought to add the charge of exposing yourself to the public," I shouted! I put her in the back of the vehicle to conceal her from all the stares of the officers that had gathered around laughing, and also from the pitiful eyes of the public. I could tell the officers were disappointed because they wanted an encore. I drove her around the block so I could talk to her in private.

As an officer working this particular task force, I had options that other officers didn't have. Lina had many contacts with officers, but she did not have any warrants for her arrest. The first thing I asked her was why was she out on the streets? Lina was like many of the young girls looking for excitement. She had the potential to be a beautiful person, but bad choices in life had led her to disrespecting her total being.

It seemed that when people get hooked on drugs one of the first things that is neglected is self-hygiene. Then they lose their motivation to be anything other than a drug addict and they eventually lose all sense of reasoning. The priority of having the drugs supercedes everything else. She didn't seem to have gotten to that point and she was a beautiful person underneath the makeup and the attitude. She was still clean and well dressed.

"Why are you out here, Lina," I ask almost demanding an answer?

"Where am I supposed to be," she retorted, "in the kitchen baking some damn cookies or cake or something?"

"How about school or work," was my come back?

"I got kicked out of school long time ago and whose gonna hire me except some hamburger joint? They ain't got no money," she boasted, "unless I do like Shanee."

"What does Shanee do," I asked?

"She works at a hamburger place, but her real money comes from selling drugs in the place," was her reply.

I talked to Lina about the effects of drugs and what they were doing to her in addition to having her act like a fool in public. Then I gave her a choice: detoxify and rehab or get arrested. She thought for a short while and then gave me her answer.

"If you don't arrest me, my brother will kill me," she said fearfully. "He will think I made a deal with the police or something."

Her brother was one of the main gangsters in the hood and was also selling drugs big time.

"Finally the truth," I replied, "so you're out here selling for your brother? What kind of brother would have his sister on the street corner selling drugs and doing the things you're doing?"

"I ain't going there at all," she responded. "Arrest me!"

"Actually, I can cite you and release you," I said.

"Hell no you ain't!" She was fuming with anger. "You better take me away from here and release me. You turn me a loose here and I'm dead. They'll swear I talked to the police."

I could see she was terribly afraid that the dealers would suspect her if she walked away after talking to me. I drove her away from the area for her own safety and cited her for possession and released her. I gave her my card and let her know that I was there if she decided to make the right choice.

The next day through investigating and knocking on doors, I was able to find out where Shanee worked. I waited until she got off and went to her house. After a long wait I was invited in. I figured she needed time to stash her stuff. Shanee was living in the projects taking care of her children and boyfriend. I talked to her in private and told her that I knew about the drugs she was selling at the hamburger stand and if she didn't put a halt to it I would take her down. I made it clear to her; if I did she would lose her housing and probably the children.

She had her boyfriend staying with her and she was supporting him. He was one of those guys that never worked and was at an intellectual level three times lower than standard. It was another one of those situations that you wonder how can a girl like that (half educated and very attractive) be with a guy like him (no education, no looks, no money, no job and no game).

"One of the good thing's that would come out of it would be you would lose that freeloading boyfriend," I said. "He probably is eating food that should be going to your kids?"

"You can say that again," she agreed. "Damn Nigger just about eating me out of house and home."

"If you need some food or clothes for the kids, here is my card. Don't hesitate to call and do it before the kids get hungry; I'm not feeding your freeloading boyfriend!" I shouted. I wanted to let her know the food wasn't coming if he was there.

A week later I went by the restaurant where Shanee worked and found out she had quit the job. She left the kids with her mama and ran off with her freeloading boyfriend. It is sad, but these are the choices being made among our young people today. They are putting their own lust and selfishness as a priority before their children and family.

Case 12: Shutdown

It was one of those days when you wake up and you just know something good is going to happen. Ted and I had been checking the knotholes in the trees at Mirasol Park looking for drug stashes. This was often the most likely place those selling the drugs would hide them. They often buried it close by or would hide it under a can or piece of debris. They would pick something that was natural to the park and use it as a hiding place to stash their drugs until a buyer came by. Then they would discreetly go to that location or have someone else go and get what was needed for the sale and complete the transaction.

There were quite a few guys at the park and you could tell this was the day to deliver. The sellers would all gather at the park on a certain day and wait for their delivery. You never knew who would be the one to deliver, but the last car to drive up was often the carrier. After the last car arrived they would eventually go to that car one at a time until everyone had received their portion.

On this particular day all the obvious sellers had disappeared but the users were still coming to the park and being serviced. One of the workers at the center would leave each day and come back after lunch with a carton of orange juice. When he was gone there was no activity, but when he returned the activity would resume.

Ted and I could see a deal going down and when we approached, the parties involved would flee into the center and the drugs would vanish when they came out on the other side. We would search them but the purchased drugs could never be found. It was obvious that the workers in the center including the elderly lady that was in charge were involved. When they went through the center they would give the drugs to someone inside and it would be stashed in a safe place.

That morning we went to the lady in charge and told her our suspicions, but instead of getting help we got a lecture. For the sake of anonymity we will call her Ms. F for Freeloader.

"Ms. F," I said, "we have followed several people in this center that we knew had just bought drugs, but when they come out on the other side its gone."

"Well, I don't know why you just don't leave these kids alone," she replied. "They're only trying to support their families."

"Say that again," said Ted, surprised at her response.

"I said why don't ya'll just leave them kids alone they're trying to support their families," she replied. She took the moment to look at each of us to see how we would respond.

She continued, "I know their mothers and they are just making it."

"First," I replied, "many of these guys are not kids, they are grown men. We just made it too in our family," I replied. "It wasn't easy for any of us, Black or Hispanic, but selling drugs was not an option in my house."

I could see that she was determined to give us a cosmetic response just to get us out of her office. Ted and I both stood up at the same time, because we knew the conversation was over.

"If we run them inside the center and you hide them then we are working against each other," I shouted.

"We, I don't work for the police, baby," she answered sarcastically.

"If you are not against the drug dealing that's going on, then you are for it," I replied.

"No, I just think ya'll should leave these kids alone," she replied. It was apparent that she was determined not to cooperate.

"Let's get one thing straight, Ms. F." I replied, "The people we're talking about are not kids. Some of them are as old as we are."

Ted interrupted, "we are not talking about selling candy, maam! We're talking drugs, which kill people or cause people to be killed. You're not helping them by allowing them to be around these younger children selling drugs."

I could see Ted was getting furious when he shouted, "you got programs going on here with the elderly people and they have to contend with your so call 'kids' hanging around outside dropping off and picking up drugs in the parking lot?"

"I still say, they ain't hurting anybody, so leave them alone" she belted.

"These kids are gonna cause you to get shut down," I replied.

"Baby, I was here before you even thought about putting on that uniform. It's gonna take somebody bigger than ya'll to shut me down," she boasted.

Her bottom line statement was she was not going to help us and as long as she was there they could continue their activities. We passed this information on to our supervisor and continued our patrol around the area.

After watching the worker go to the store each day and purchase a carton of orange juice, then visit some of the dealers, we thought there was a connection, but we couldn't figure it out. It was hard to see any exchange take place from our surveillance position.

One evening after this worker had left for the day it was strange that he always took the same carton of orange juice with him. I could drink a carton of juice in about thirty seconds, but it took him all day.

Ted and I continued patrolling the area, going to meetings and helping out where ever we could. Ms. F. didn't have much to do with us and we got the message that she had been there for so long she was almost untouchable. I thought the only way we are going to get her attention is by a miracle. So I prayed, "Lord send a miracle in our direction."

One day we detected a transaction between a couple of younger players. We knew the kid by name and chased him into the center. Ms. F. came out and wanted to know what the commotion was about. She took the liberty to tell us that this kid was not involved in drugs and that we should leave him alone. We had apprehended him just as he started to exit one of the doors. We searched him and found nothing. We knew that he was always in our sight and he didn't have time to give it to any one. I continued talking to him and Ted started to trace his tracks. He went back over the route the kid took as he ran through the center.

"Damn!" said Ted as he bent and picked something off the ground. "What the hell!"

"What you got," I said, thinking he may have found some cash that was dumped.

"Colt!" he shouted. "He's ten-fifteen (10-15)." This was the code for being under arrest. He approached me with his hand out and resting in the palm of his hand was the largest single piece of crack cocaine I had ever seen. We were both astonished because we had walked by it thinking it was something else because of its size. Most pieces of crack have been broken in pieces valued at about twenty dollars. This was indeed an oddity. The size of it made it a $500 piece of crack.

We called our supervisor and the head of the Urban League who had the responsibility of the Recreation Center through Parks and Recreation Department.

We begin searching the premises only where the suspect had access. We were shown the various places he had been earlier and in one of the rooms there was a refrigerator. Ted checked it out and there was a familiar carton of orange juice. I picked it up and looked inside to make sure it was orange juice, and it was. I returned the item to its place and Ted asked, "Did you check the refrigerator?"

"Yeah, but you can check it again," I said.

This was something we did, rechecking each other. Sometimes I would check something he had already checked and would find something he missed. He would do the same for me and would find something I missed. It was our own check and balance system.

I noticed Ted shaking the carton and something started to rattle.

"Orange juice doesn't rattle," he said. He looked at the worker who the carton belonged to and asked, "What's in here?"

"Nothing man," said the worker, "just orange juice. It might be some ice inside," he responded.

"How long has it been inside the refrigerator," Ted inquired?

"Just a few minutes," said the worker.

"No it isn't cold enough to have ice inside," said Ted. "So you wouldn't mind if I poured it out and checked?"

"Hell yeah I would," he exclaimed. "Ya'll gonna buy me some more juice?"

"How about we give you the money and you can buy it yourself," I replied?

At this point you could see that something was wrong. The worker started to get nervous. I made sure he watched as Ted did his thing with the juice. He poured it from one container into another and stuck to the bottom of the carton was a few pieces of alleged crack cocaine. He then took a piece of cloth, which served as a screen and poured the contents of both containers onto the cloth and there resting on the cloth were twenty-one pieces of crack cocaine. At $20-$25 a piece, he had about $500 worth of crack in his orange juice container. Our suspicions of the worker were true. He was supplying and he was making his contacts when he went to lunch. His orange juice carton was only a means for transporting drugs from one point to the other.

We placed him under arrest and stopped at that point. This thing was bigger than the both of us. We called our supervisor down and also the Urban League supervisor. We got permission from the City Parks and Recreation and from the necessary personnel and did a complete search of the premises. When we were done the center was shut down. Ms. F. was asked to take an early retirement but decided to fight her case. When she returned to work the following Monday, the locks had been changed and she was not allowed to enter the building.

Things got a lot better because the police had the freedom to come and go. The Urban League took charge of the Center and replaced Ms. F. Eventually Ms. F. was band from the center, but she had been there so long they showed their respect for her and retired her. The Center was later relocated and is doing fine without the complexion of drugs surrounding it. I thank God because the so-called untouchable was touched and this was the beginning of a great change. I know the powers above allowed us to see that "Miracles do happen!" Thanks to Mr. Clark and others we were able to get the right people inside working with the kids instead of someone that had become codependent and were justifying this sort of activity.

Case 13: Why do some people use crack?

I think everyone has a story as to why they started using drugs: frustration, adversities in life, pressures of society, some were tricked, others were trying to avoid peer pressure, and of course, curiosity. I was told by a female and a male that they started using crack because they wanted to lose weight. They stated they had been around people using different kinds of drugs, but it was evident those using crack cocaine showed immediate signs of weight loss.

They both stated after dieting and taking pills and never getting the results they wanted they decided to use crack cocaine. After a couple of uses they were chasing a high that could never be duplicated. They needed more crack to get to where they were the time before. It was the quickest habit forming drug ever used. They were successful in losing weight, but they also lost a sense of hygiene, self respect, their home, job and family. They both admitted it was a habit that may one day cost them their lives.

One female subject lived in the projects and had children. She felt it necessary to lose weight by any means possible, so with her welfare money, she started buying crack cocaine. She figured by losing weight she would be more attractive to men. Now she realizes that having a drug habit makes you even less attractive. Some men would have no problem with a woman overweight, but no one's wants a drug addict.

Another male subject stated, "Man all these crack addicts seem to be cut (thin and muscular). I thought if I tried it for a few months I could get the same muscular definition. Shit, I still ain't where I want to be and now I'm hooked on crack."

I replied, "If you had the chance to go back, would you?"

"Hell yeah, I'd rather be fat than hooked on crack any day."

One of the most unusual reasons came from a person that was a computer technician. He travelled all over the United States and made nearly six figures a year. He had friends that had used drugs and had lost everything. He saw the lack of control they had and how the drugs control them and immediate caused them to spiral downwards. He felt they were weak and pathetic, and if they had will power at all they should be able to overcome the addiction. He felt it was just a matter of temperance. He stated that no drug can cause a person to go down that fast and that these were weak individuals from the start. He felt that a strong willed person could take the drug and be strong enough to fight the addiction, if he chose to do so. It was a matter of mind over matter. He made a bet with his friends that he could use the drug and quit when he felt like it.

He volunteered and after one time he was hooked on crack cocaine. He lost his job, home, respect and family within a few months. This was ten years ago and the last time I heard he was still begging family members for money to buy drugs, and his family had considered him an outcast because they could not trust him in their presence. He would break into their homes every chance he got and steal anything that wasn't tied down.

I seen him living at the park on several occasions, and I spoke with him and gave him money to get food. He advised me that he was looking for a job and would spend the money on a ride to get to an interview. His sister in another state had heard about his condition and was concerned. She sent him money to go to New Mexico and live with her, but after a few months he was thrown out again. He should have never underestimated the power of the drug, or have been so foolish to even try such a challenge. He is now paying the price for losing. He was right about temperance being an effective solution, but avoidance would have better, when dealing with drugs.

Crack cocaine and crystal meth are a two of the most addictive drugs on the streets and using them is a death sentence for many people. I have seen users turn against their father and mother, sister and brother, wife and children, and friends and relatives. The saddest thing is they turn against themselves. I heard an individual say once, **"you wish you were dead, but you're afraid to die."**

I must admit I had a misperception of crack users after talking to these few individuals. Ted and I were involved in surveillance at one of the suspected drug areas, when we saw two men under a tree openly smoking crack from a distance. We waited for the opportune time and closed in on them. They both started running away, but they decided to stop after hearing our commands to put their hands up. When we searched them we found nothing, but on the ground we found a crack pipe. Of course, neither one would claim ownership. One was overweight and the other was skinny and frail.

"Well," I stated, "there is no question who this belongs too."

"Yeah," said Ted, "let me see, the fat guy or the skinny guy."

Since he was the closest to the crack pipe we gave the skinny guy the honors. When we separated them and began to question them I was surprised when the skinny suspect stated he wanted to talk to me in private.

"Officer Colter," he said, "I know you are a minister, and I want you to know the truth, and I believe you will listen to me. You have a misperception that needs to be corrected."

"What is that," I responded?

"If you think only skinny people smoke crack you're wrong. Both of you guys are wrong about me, but I'm going to set the record straight."

"Well," I replied, "set the record straight."

"You guys have prejudged me because of my size or because of the way I look," he whispered. "If my buddy won't step up then I guess I will have to take the rap, but that is not my crack pipe. I have smoked crack in the past, but not today and not recently. I want you to know that fat people smoke crack too."

He was right, I should not have judged him, and I had previously been told that people were using crack as a dumb excuse to lose weight.

I ask Ted if he would watch this guy, while I talked with the fat guy, and he agreed to do so.

The subject seemed relieved that we had accused the skinny guy with possession of drug paraphernalia. I approached him saying, "Your buddy told me you guys are friends and he is willing to take the rap for the crack pipe. I wonder if we would have accused you, would you have taken the rap for him? I guess you still have a true friend that is willing to go to jail for you."

"He said he would take the rap for the crack pipe," he inquired? Man I can't let that happen. That dude hasn't smoked in weeks. He was just hanging out here with me shooting the breeze. That pipe is mine and I was the one actually smoking, not him."

"How do I know if you're not just trying to cover for him," I countered?

"If I tell you something will you give me a break," he pleaded. "It will be enough to set my buddy free?"

"What kind of break are we talking about," I responded?

"It don't matter," he interrupted, "just check my left shoe. I got a piece of crack there. That proves I'm the one using, not my buddy."

I checked his shoe and found the crack. I asked him if he would be willing to go to rehab rather than jail, and he accepted. We set his friend free with a verbal reprimand, and took the guilty party directly to rehab.

His friend came to the car and said, "I would have taken the rap dog; I had your back. I've been there before homes; this is your first time, and you don't need this on your record."

I asked him, "have you ever been arrested before," and he stated "no sir." I asked him why he started using, and he stated he was just curious, plus, he needed to lose some pounds.

Case: 14: Rats and Roaches

Two things I hate dealing with are rats and roaches. I had a complaint from a lady about her boyfriend who was no longer at the residence, and she wanted an officer to respond. The incident had taken place an hour prior to her reporting it. Since I had the area, I took the call.

My Sergeant warned me earlier about the same residence, stating he had been run out by the infestation of roaches. When I arrived she invited me into her apartment and it was dark. Apparently her electricity was turned off. I had to turn on my flashlight, because it had become an "officer safety" issue. I didn't care for interviewing a person in a dark room. She said she and her boyfriend had a fight and he had broken a couple of things in the house and she wanted to report the damage. While interviewing her I could see with peripheral vision a hole in her wall. I kept the light on her as we talked.

"Did he knock the hole in the wall," I asked.

"What hole," she responded? "There's no hole in the wall."

I turned and shined my light on the wall and the wall was covered with roaches. The numerous roaches that had covered the wall in the darkness gave it the dark appearance of a hole in the wall.

"Oh that," she said, "I threw my plate at him and it must have splattered food on the wall and the roaches decided to clean it up."

In a split second the roaches were gone out of the room, but not out of my mind. I ended my interview and as I walked from the room I could hear a crunching sound beneath my feet, and when I looked down, my shoes were covered with roaches and I had stepped on several as I made my exit.

I then responded to an abandon residence where it was allegedly being occupied by transients or drug addicts. They were trespassing and the owner wanted them removed. I arrived and waited for my backup. There were two individuals lying on the floor, and the roaches ran for cover when I entered. There were human feces in the corner of the room and that was designated as their self made rest room area; they had also feces and urine collected in a bucket to dispose of whenever they decided it was too disgusting and odiferous. During the interview I was told that they would take the defecation and urine and bury it in the desert at night. After checking them out for warrants and advising them of their violations, I cited them and asked them to leave. I continued to check the residence and was shocked when in one of the rooms it appeared the floor was moving in the dark. I shined my light into the room and the floor was covered with rats. Now I had the thought of rats occupying my mind along with the roaches.

I called to Ted who was assisting me and was checking the perimeter, and we decided to call the Health Department. They sent out a representative and within a couple of hours the place was condemned. They even sent a dozer out the next day and the place was demolished. Rats and roaches were scattering from the area, and so did I. It is appalling and atrocious the conditions that people will live in. Drugs can bring you down to the pits of despair and to the depths of hell if you allow it to do so. I had seen enough rats and roaches to last me for a lifetime, or should I say until the next shift.

Chapter VII
Gang Unit

I transferred to the Gang Unit and work there for about five years, but they still had me working on the Southside. It is believed that the average education level of gang members at this time was about Junior High School. It certainly was evident that we were not dealing with rocket scientist. They were very tough until you arrested one of them and immediately they would cry for their mothers. Even those in their 20's and 30's would ask for their mothers.

We arrested one of the notorious individuals in the neighborhood who was in his 30's. The first thing he said was "call my mother." Before we could oblige him, she was already at the scene wanting to know what we were going to do with her baby. She knew he was selling drugs and she kept asking if there was something in the house that he wanted her to keep, before we locked the trailer where he was living. It was obvious she was referring to his stash or his money. He knew we were on to what was being asked so he played it cool, volunteered to come without an incident and told her everything was ok. We were there to arrest him, not to search his residence, unless there was something in plain view.

On one occasion we knew that her son was selling drugs behind her home and through surveillance we confirmed this. We were surprised when she called the police informing us that there were dealers behind her home and she wanted them arrested. When we arrived they had vacated the area. I spoke to one of my informants and he stated she didn't like the idea that other dealers were taking over her son's spot. She wanted us to clear them out so she could claim the spot, so her son could continue his venture close to home.

I worked with the gang Unit for five years and I believe that what we did was very instrumental in getting many of the players off the streets. I learned that many gangsters considered themselves to be religious and I believe they are, but they did not have a relationship with God. There are many religious people in this world who have no relationship with God.

I remember one day being parked next to a beautiful Catholic Church trying to catch up on paper work. I observed a vehicle carrying several young Mexican juveniles. Each of them blessed themselves with the sign of the cross and said a prayer while parked at the red light then the vehicle moved on. After about fifteen minutes a call came out on the air describing a vehicle that had been involved in a drive by shooting. I responded to the scene and learned that it was the same vehicle I had seen earlier. Apparently it was fitting for them to pray and ask for Mother Mary's blessings while in route to a drive-bye shooting.

I have also attended funeral services and wakes (or viewings) of alleged gang members. I noticed how the victims are portrayed in death like angels. I have seen family members sitting in front of a casket that was adorned with gang rags and emblems containing gang colors. The victim while lying in the casket was wearing gang clothing and gang colors. I peered into the casket to see the deceased and noticed gang rags, gang emblems and a small bag of marijuana, which someone had put inside near a crucifix or a rosary. Many of the people attending were clad in gag attire or wearing T-Shirts written in gangster script as a memorial to the victim. As they passed by the casket they gave their gang signs to the deceased and some stood in anticipation that he would return the sign; then the famous quote, "See you later Homes, in heaven."

I wonder about parents that would allow such a sacred moment to become a sacrilege. What are they learning in church to make them think they can lie; cheat, steal and kill, and they all will meet up in heaven? I wonder why the parents of kids who are in gangs don't buy life insurance for them. If they did some families would be very wealthy. I am not being facetious I am being truthful. It seems that the very people you come to for donations to bury your child are the victims of the violence caused by this very person. It is frequent that the deceased is uninsured and the family and friends are doing car washes and yard sales to get enough money to give them a decent burial.

I told kids in the classes I taught on Gang Resistance Education and Training, when you join a gang you just gave every gang member in the opposing gang a license to kill any member of your family. You gave them a reason and permission to do a drive-bye on your little sister or brother. You have opened the door for them to point their guns at your parents and friends.

I tell a "wanna be" gang member that there is no such thing as a "wanna be" to an opposing gang member. If you look like a gangster they treat you like one.

When you're walking down the streets after school and you have on your gang attire, and some opposing gang member drives by, he don't pull out his gun and ask you if you are a wanna be or a real gang member. He just starts shooting.

I told a story to the kids in class about "Decoys." When I was a young we had our shotguns, BB guns and rifles that our parents had allowed us to use to go hunting in the desert. One day we came upon a pond full of ducks. We took our time and inched our way closer to the pond so we all could be in range to shoot the ducks. When we felt we were close enough, I informed the rest of the group that we would all shoot at the same time. We noticed that some of the ducks flew away but others remained. I thought it was rather strange that the remaining ducks allowed us to get so close to them without being spooked. Each person had their sights on a particular duck in the pond and when I gave them the ok, they started shooting. The guns blasting, the smoke rising and the noise we made must have sounded like the Battle of Gettysburg. When the smoke cleared and some of us were out of bullets, the firing ceased and now it was time to collect our birds.

We observed an interesting sight. There were ducks floating around in that pool upright with their wings and heads shot off. We were so excited that some of them reloaded and started shooting again until I made them all stop. We just couldn't understand what kind of ducks could stand up to such firepower. While standing there in total disbelief the owner of the pond came by because he had heard what sounded like a war going on. He started yelling and screaming at us saying, "Damn kids you done shot up all my decoys!"

We ran for our lives and when we were able to stop and catch our breath one of my friends said he wanted to go back and get his duck. When we asked him what kind of a duck is a decoy, he said there are several kinds of ducks and a decoy was a type of duck. He said there are mallards, Blue Grosse and Decoys. It wasn't until we got home that we learn from our elders it was a fake duck.

The point to this story is that a decoy is like a "wanna be" gang member. If you look like a duck, float like a duck, hanging around the pond with ducks, you will get shot like a duck.

One of the most effective methods we had in cleaning up the streets was called "The Trojan Horse" raid. We would get a van from the postal service or one of the local businesses. All the gang unit officers, which were approximately eight officers, would dress in our raid jackets and drive around to the local projects and street corners where they were openly selling drugs. Most of our raids were done under the cover of darkness. Sometimes there would be up to ten people hanging out at a corner or in a certain alley. They would flash their cigarette lighters (or flick their bic) at the customers acknowledging they were ready for business. Our surveillance would watch and let us know where the dealers were stashing their drugs. They would never have the drugs on them, but would have it close by. If they made contact with someone they would go to their stash *(As I have said before It was normally wrapped in plastic and buried in the ground, place under the hood of a car, put under trash cans, in the knotholes in trees or the crevice between two branches, or hid in some discrete place close by).* On some occasions, someone nearby who appeared to be detached from the group would be holding it. We would blink our lights and then turn them off as we drove up slowly pretending to be a customer. The van had sliding doors, which allowed everyone to bail out in an instant. When the server(s) came up to the van we would bail out and grab someone. We were dressed in bright orange colored raid jackets and had flashlights that seemed to light up the whole neighborhood. It was like dropping a cat down in the middle of a bunch of rats or turning on the lights at a roach picnic. They scattered in all directions. Some ran into each other, into walls, shrubbery and sometimes right into our arms. Normally we had to chase them down but often we could arrest ten people a night due to "Trojan Horse" raids.

The Gang Unit was always doing raids on houses for drugs. Crack, Marijuana, Crystal Meth and Heroin were the drugs mostly involved.

Before every raid our Sergeant would tell us to double tie our shoelaces. He would tell the story about officers tripping because their shoelaces came untied. This became his pet pea. Many of the officers thought it was childish, but I don't ever remember anyone tripping. We did go to a couple of wrong houses, but we never tripped.

Our Sergeant had been my Sergeant while in the Task Force and now he was over the Gang Unit. It appeared to me that the Department seemed to have it out for him. It was obvious by the way he was treated. I do know that we probably put more gangsters, drug dealers and users off the street than any other unit other than those actually working narcotics. I think his only problem was he wasn't prejudice, bias or a bigot like some of the others. He had a rapport with minorities and the people in the community respected him so that didn't go over very well with the Command Staff. The fact that he knew many of the Black and Mexican families gave him some insight on what was going on in the neighborhoods. He also knew many of the gangsters and drug dealers from their childhood. The other problem he had was that he cared for the people that worked under him. I guess from the position of Sergeant and up many of them stop looking at the people under them and are always looking at those above for promotions. I have lost a many of good friends once they got promoted. They seem to fall off the edge of the world into a place called "Stuck-up Valley."

I remember on one occasion when some of the gangsters had barricaded themselves in their home after a confrontation with officers. They refused to talk to anyone except the Sergeant and myself. I wasn't available but he was. He went over and resolved the conflict without anyone getting shot. That incident was quickly forgotten among the Command Staff. He was also instrumental in helping the neighborhood groups literally clean up their neighborhood.

I learned many things about the Administration and how they operate. I would assume that any officer reading this would probably agree with me. The Police Department would put certain people in certain positions and it seemed that things were going fine. When everything is going well and people are getting along and are effective that is when the Department decides to change things. The Administration gets nervous when things are going well. They never want anyone to get comfortable in their job assignment. I was told as a child, "if it isn't broken don't try to fix it." The Department at times did just the opposite: "if it was working then its time to break it up or change it." This organization had a reputation for fixing what wasn't broken.

I don't know how many times we had to change something that was working for us. If we had a Commander or Supervisor that was well liked and doing an excellent job, then watch out. You could count on that person being transferred.

While in the Gang Unit, my supervisor changed four times. While on a certain task force it changed three times and in the SRO program it changed four times. It was hard to keep up because they were changing and each one had a different concept about how thing should be done. Many of them were good supervisors. It's just that the position kept turning over. What was in this week was out next week.

The job initially involved being out on the front lines, gathering intelligence, issuing search warrants, preventing shootings and mediating with feuding gangs and being proactive. We worked our cases, presented them to the Grand Jury and issued them through the County Attorney's Office. After I left the Unit, the focus changed and Gang Unit officers were sitting in the office and going out once in a while only to do speaking engagements. I can say that under the supervision of two of the Supervisors we did get some things done. These are some of those cases. The names have been changed in most cases, again to protect the guilty.

Case 1: The Big E

I remember when the Big E was a Little E and was trying to go to school. He was constantly hanging out at the projects on the Southside around relatives and other drug dealers. All it takes is for a kid in the neighborhood to start making a little money and he forgets about school and family. That is why I never bought the story about the poor kids from the neighborhoods dealing drugs to take care of their families. There were many more cases where those so-called unfortunate kids exploited their mom, dad and the rest of their family. They sold the poison to their own brothers and sisters and many of the parents never received a dime from them. Many parents did not condone their children out selling drugs or advocate their violent behavior, so the perception that the parents were all involved is a lie.

Gang members never seem to disconnect from their mother's apron strings. It didn't matter what time of night or day, when they got their one phone call the first word out of their mouth was, "MAMA!" Sometimes I wondered where some of the mothers were when their children were becoming gangsters and drug dealers. I am reminded of the scripture that says, *"The rod and reproof give wisdom: but a child left to himself bringeth his mother to shame"* (Proverb 29:15, KJV).

The young people today have no respect for themselves or their parents, the bible tells us, *"There is a generation that curseth their father, and doth not bless their mother"* (Proverb 30:11, KJV)… *"There is a generation, whose teeth are as swords, and their jaw teeth as knives, to devour the poor from off the earth, and the needy from among men"* (Proverb 30:14, KJV).

Big E was one of those kids I saw grow up into crime. He was allegedly responsible for the killing of his mother's boyfriend by hitting him over the head with an orange juice bottle and all the witnesses refused to testify against him. An eyewitness that refused to testify gave the police this information. He terrified many of the helpless and hopeless people in the neighborhood. He was like many of the small time dealers; they kept their money in their pockets or in the car or they spent it as soon as they made it.

He was involved in child molesting, shootings, rape and whatever crime that was available. He had one small characteristic that set him off from among the others. We found out what it was after he had raped a couple of young girls. They called him "the five second kid" and described his penis as short as his action. Like many gangster's he could not standup by himself and always had an entourage with him everywhere he went. The very family members that started him out selling drugs were now buying from him and selling for him.

I would go and visit his grandmother who seemed like a nice elderly lady who didn't have a clue about her grandson. It was different with his mother. She was dependant on his drug money and never corrected any of his negative behavior. She refused to say anything about the killing of her boyfriend for fear of her own son.

He was very street smart like many of the young dealers, but they couldn't tell you who the president was and probably had to have someone count their money for them.

This guy had more fourteen and fifteen year olds pregnant, because that was the age he could relate to intellectually. We were able to send some of his friends away for murder and that cooled him off for a while. When I left the unit he had went into hibernation like a bear in the winter. His entourage had been arrested one by one and he probably felt naked without them.

Usually when the dealers disappear they normally reappeared on the Eastside. At that time it was the least infested area of the city, but now it's like all the rest of the city. It has its share of both gangsters and drug dealers.

The sad thing about Big E and many others is that they hadn't done anything else in life but sell drugs. They didn't have an education and many of them exhibited a learning disability of a sort. They had been in this mess for so long they probably couldn't fill out an application for McDonalds. If by some means they did, I doubt if they had the skills to read the list that showed how a person wanted their burger. That is how sad our children have become who have conceded to selling drugs as a means of making a living.

The big E's last known total of children he fathered was nine and rising. The sad thing is that many of his victims were, so called church girls; girl raised up in the church.

Case 2: The Cat Spirit

There are many strange things that policeman encounter on the job. If you are unaware of the spiritual warfare that is occurring in this world, you will write off many encounters as just strange. There are those phenomenons that many officers just can't explain so they come up with their own explanation. There are powers of darkness and evil spirits in this world and you had better be aware when you go on certain calls. Apostle Paul wrote:

- **Ephesians 6:12**: "For we wrestle not against flesh and blood, but against principalities, against powers, against the rulers of the darkness of this world, against spiritual wickedness in high places" **(KJV).**
- **2 Corinthians 10:3-5:** [3]For though we walk in the flesh, we do not war after the flesh: [4](For the weapons of our warfare are not carnal, but mighty through God to the pulling down of strong holds;) [5]Casting down

91

imaginations, and every high thing that exalteth itself against the knowledge of God, and bringing into captivity every thought to the obedience of Christ…" **(KJV).**

My Sergeant was briefing the gang officers about an encounter he had with a person that was involved in satanic worship and cultic practices. A member of the family began to act like a cat and while sounding like a cat the person was making motions with their hands like a cat pawing and scratching at its victim or opponent. She came towards him screeching and hissing and trying to scratch him with her fingernails. The officers with him subdued the person and the situation was resolved by a couple of arrest. The Sergeant was beleaguered by the event and it was obvious he would never forget. When we heard the story many of the officers laughed about it, except for me and another Black officer. We knew that Satan is busy and there are spirits in this world that you better not take lightly.

A couple of days later Rob [other Black officer] and I were doing a surveillance of an alleged crack house on the Northside. It was dark so we contacted the unit and told them we were going in on foot to better assess the situation. This was very dangerous because Rob was very tall and well known in the neighborhood. I was a minister and while working in the Mirasol Task Force my picture had been in the paper and on TV a few times while I was in uniform. We decided with the cover of darkness we could get away with it if we stayed in the shadows. One of the known prostitutes being high on drugs approached us while we were conversing in the yard with others and recognized us.

"Ooowee," she said, "I know who ya'll are. Ya'll the police!" she screamed, "Hey, ya'll, these guys are the police!"

Immediately, Rob interrupted. "This girl must be tripping or something," he said to our company that was now apprehensive.

"She's gotta be out of her mind," I said to the guy next to me.

He replied, "Get your sorry ass outta here girl we're trying do business."

"Damn, girl you are tripping," said one of the guys, "you ain't never seen two Black policeman together in Tucson."

They then tried to sale us what looked like the chalk inside of a board of sheetrock, but we refused. Then it was a regular rock off the ground. We knew they had something because one of the guys in the unit had previously made a buy. After a while it was apparent they were scamming the buyers, and they hadn't received their load for the night. We had already made a couple of buys from that address earlier that evening, so we decided to call in the troops. We were able to somehow click a signal to the unit and let them know to come in. We continued casually talking to the guys out front and trying to ignore Roslyn [prostitute] who was now sounding like a cat and beginning to hiss as she started towards Rob.

"I know you, you're Rob and you're the preacher man!" She yelled.

She then opened her mouth wide and started grimacing; her fingers were spread apart like a cat ready to claw something. The sound coming from her was ghastly, like a cat backed against a wall, and you could see she was possessed with some unnatural spirit. She reached for Rob and he tossed her to the ground and at the same time I was trying to put my hand over her mouth so she would shut up. She was scratching and hissing and was able to stand up, but Rob did a slam-dunk on her that Michael Jordan would have been proud to do. The guys got suspicious and started backing away. Our backup arrived immediately and everyone scattered with officers in raid jackets chasing after them.

Rob and I were on the ground with Roslyn [cat girl] and were able to put cuffs on her. White liquid started coming from her mouth when she vomited. She kept screaming and clawing like a cat. The Unit was able to contain the residence and detained as many of the alleged suspects as possible. One of them was a prostitute and a friend of Roslyn's.

"Is she sick or something," I asked Roslyn's friend referring to Roslyn vomiting?

"Hell no, she ain't sick like you think, but she damn sho' [sure] is sick," she replied. "Look at her, damn; you know what that is that is coming out of her?"

"No I don't, and I don't care to know," I said.

"Man that's semen she is throwing up," she shouted.

"Semen," I retorted.

"Yeah, semen or whatever you wanna to call it. She has been doing oral sex with one guy after another and she is a semen freak," said the female. "The girl doesn't use protection or nothing. That's what's coming out of her. She loves the stuff!"

She turned and walked away pulling my arm along with her and saying, "Lets get away from her this shit is making me sick. I seen her do this before and it's disgusting."

No one wanted to even touch Roslyn after that, but she was arrested for paraphernalia. We were able to get signed permission to search the apartment. The lessee was an elderly Black man that was enjoying the free crack while allowing the dealers and users to use his apartment. He smelled as if he hadn't bathed in a year and he was sitting in a chair that he never moved from except to go to the bathroom. Many of those that had been detained agreed with his statement.

"That's one funky dude," said one of the detainees, "funky to the bone."

"If I was ya'll I wouldn't have him move because that man stinks," said another of the detainees. "If he moves nothing will come from him but funk."

We begin to look around and roaches covered the furniture, the walls and even covered the ceiling. As we were searching the roaches were falling from the ceiling on our heads and shoulders. We could feel roaches in our hair and it made us apprehensive about looking up.

We made the old man get up from the chair so we could see if he was sitting on anything, but when he arose the smell was so odiferous we had to move the pillows he sat on with our night sticks and take them outside to air out. Several guys had to run out of the apartment to keep from vomiting inside. We had the pleasure of opening the refrigerator and stove and looking inside. There was rotted meat and spoiled food in both. Some of the meat in the stove had maggots coming out of it. The refrigerator had cups of old sodas and drinks that had been there so long the ingredients had separated inside the container. The milk had clabbered and poured out in lumps. No one was able to continue the search because of the condition of the apartment was horrendous. Roaches falling into our hair, the stench of the whole apartment, the rotted food and spoiled items that had been left behind for weeks was too much for us.

The Sergeant called off the search and we had the Health Department come over and the placed was condemned.

We contacted Roslyn's mother and advised her of the condition of her daughter, but she refused to get involved. She totally disowned her child. It made me wonder if her relationship with her mother and step father was a source of her problems. She had been of the streets for years as a juvenile. What was it that brought her to this fate? Since Roslyn was eighteen there was nothing more we could do except take her to jail. That was a difficult task when you don't want to touch her, but the gloves saved us.

I had the opportunity to talk with her for a while in the police car as I gathered her information. I asked her if she had a million dollars what steps would she take to care for herself.

She responded, "Shit, I would go buy a million dollar piece of crack, the biggest rock in the world, and my friends and I would smoke it until it was gone."

I guess that was a foolish question to ask a foolish person. The bible tells us quite a lot about foolish people and their character. It didn't matter how much I talked to her she answered foolishly. The bible says, *"The way of a fool is right in his own eyes, but he who heeds counsel is wise"* (Proverbs 12:15, NKJV) and that, *"a wise man fears and departs from evil, but a fool rages and is self-confident"* (NKJV, Proverbs 14:16). *"As a dog returneth to his vomit, so a fool returneth to his folly"* (Proverbs 26:11, KJV).

The parent of such a person must grieve often, for it is written, *"He that begetteth a fool doeth it to his sorrow: and the father of a fool hath no joy"* (Proverbs 17:21, KJV).

If a foolish person would just shut their mouth their intellect could be concealed momentarily. The word of God says, *"A fool's mouth is his destruction and his lips are the snare of his soul"* (Proverbs 18:7 KJV), *"…and Speak not in the ears of a fool: for he will despise the wisdom of thy words"* (Proverbs 23:9, KJV).

What is there to be done and why do they continue to return to their mess. God's word mentions the correction for a foolish person: *A whip for the horse, a bridle for the ass, and a rod for the fool's back"* (Proverbs 26:3, KJV).

I knew Roslyn's condition was brought on because of her addiction to drugs and that (addiction) takes away your ability to reason. I asked her about her relationship with her mother and she said her mother was too busy trying to please her step father and she didn't fit in. We as parent have a responsibility to our children and any stepmother or stepfather than requires you to desert your children isn't worth having.

I saw Roslyn on many occasions and she was always under the influence of some drug. She had neglected her hygiene and was losing all sense of reality. She was having sex for her drugs and committing petty crimes to support herself. I believe that one day she will be found dead or she will be committed to an institution of some sort for her own safety. Drug addiction is one of the greatest strongholds Satan has on people; it destroys the mind and body.

You can't help but think of your own children when you see many of the youths in the streets like Roslyn. Satan is trying to get a grip on our youth, because they are the avenues to the heart of America. We as parents must fight for what belongs to us and our children belong to us. Parents, fight for your children with all your heart, soul and spirit.

Case 3: Gousto with no gusto

It appeared that whenever there was a shooting in certain areas of town, at certain nightclubs or disturbances among the teen swingers of the city, a certain name kept popping up. We will call this subject Gousto to protect the guilty.

He was one of those immigrants that came over on a boat from Cuba when they released all their undesirables from prison and sent them to this country. He was sent to us courtesy of Fidel Castro. He was tall, dark and perverted. It seemed that he could talk young girls into being his slave if he so desired. He would rape and molest the girls and have them thinking it was their fault. None of them wanted to testify against him and when they tried, it seemed that at the last minute they would change their minds. He had a fear factor going for him that would have made Saddam Hussein jealous and envious.

He seemed to be a step ahead of us and it wasn't because of his intelligence, but due to the fear that the victims had of him. On one occasion we (gang unit officers) talked to one victim who was a very beautiful Mexican girl about seventeen years old. She stated she had been dating him via meeting him at a nightclub. Gousto was close to thirty years old, but hung around the teen joints. In fact, we really didn't know how old he was, but he was indeed older than his peers. The young lady said he had forced himself on her and when she tried to stop him he had a premature orgasm on her clothing. He then told her it was all her fault, because he loved her so much he couldn't control himself. He finally convinced her to have sex with him, but when she saw the abnormal color of the fluid that came from his body, which was disgusting, she refused. As for as Gousto was concerned this was a point of no return. He then raped her and told her if she told anyone he would kill her. The victim started apologizing to us as if it was her fault that he raped her.

Again, emphasizing to her that it was all her fault for getting him all sizzling and riled, Gousto then put a gun up to her head and made her promise not to tell anyone. He took her home and made friends with her parents, which made her situation even worst. She said she would not testify against him in court for fear of what he might do to her family. As a result of having sex with him she contracted an STD (sexually transmitted disease) that was incurable and would prevent her from having children.

The investigation led us to an apartment complex on the eastside of town. There we found a buddy of his that said Gousto was psychotic and would have no reservation about killing anyone that stood in his way. He said he had put an automatic weapon to his head and tried to make him have oral sex with him. He said he refused and Gousto left him alone after warning him not to tell anyone. I found that hard to believe.

We then followed his trail to a nightclub where he was showing a great deal of money and drugs to those associated with him. He later got into a shootout with several guys and left before the police arrived. The trail led me to a topless dance place on Miracle Mile that I must admit had some of the most beautiful women dancing there than any other places we had been in. One in particular said she knew him and had dated him. I made an appointment to see her the next day down at the police station and she agreed she would meet me there.

I will call her Princess for the sake of giving her a name. She came to the lobby the next day and waited for me to invite her into the office. I escorted her to an interview room and every officer that saw her starred uncontrollably as she walked by. Some of them spilled their drinks or dropped whatever substance they had in their hands, because they were focused on Princess. She was extremely beautiful and she knew it. I think she got more attention walking to the interview room from the officers than when she danced at the club.

It was almost impossible to interview her because every couple of minutes someone would come into the room with some lame excuse just to see her. All the men were salivating and probably half the women in the station. I was able to make light of what was happening and asked her if she had this response everywhere she went? She laughed and said, "Yes, just about." The way she was sitting seemed to get the officers attention because her dress didn't cover very much and she continued crossing and uncrossing her legs. I was told once by an old friend that the two worst things a man had to watch out for was money and a woman sitting with her legs open.

Princess had long Black hair and was about five feet seven inches tall with a beautiful complexion and a smile that matched. She was extremely shapely and probably could have made millions as a fashion model. She would have been the perfect Cinderella in a movie role. She dressed like someone out of a fashion magazine and carried herself in a very dignified manner. She said she had met a guy that she wanted to marry, who had a business and was a professional of a sort, either a lawyer or a doctor. She had dated Gousto and he threatened to tell her fiancé about their relationship if she didn't have sex with him. After having sex with him, he put a Mac-10 automatic weapon to her head and threatened to kill her. When I confronted her about having sex with him she said he was good in bed and she didn't mind. At that point her intelligence meter dropped to about zero on my scale. All she had to do now was to pull out a cigarette and the meter would have gone into the minus column. She said she would not testify against him, but she had a roommate that hated him and she might testify if she was interviewed. I scheduled an appointment to talk to her roommate and when I asked which one of the guys wanted to go with me, I think every officer raised their hands.

A few days later I went to her apartment and was invited in. This time I was the one gawking because her roommate was even more beautiful than Princess. On my list of most beautiful women in the world, she had to be in the top two. She confirmed that Gousto had come in and actually pointed the gun at both of them. She didn't want to get involved because she believed he was psycho and sadistic. She described the weapon as the one that everyone was talking about and the mire fact that he had an automatic weapon was in violation. He was a felon that had been arrested in Cuba, but here we hadn't proven anything against him. There were no witnesses that wanted to testify.

We later found out that he had raped or molested several juveniles and that was our motivation to try and get him off the streets. We took statements and had approximately thirteen girls that had been raped or molested by Gousto. Each of them was telling us sad stories about how he was treated in prison and that he had marks over his body from the torture and abuse he received in a Cuban prison. Some were so naïve they were having sex with him out of pity. He was so manipulative that they thought they were doing themselves a big favor by having sex with him.

I was busy working an investigation when I heard over the air that they had arrested him and was bringing him down to the station for an interview. It was a shock to see this pathetic looking guy who appeared to be dressed for the 70's with alligator shoes and intoxicated. It was obvious that Gousto had no gusto. His demeanor towards women was that they were something to be used by men for pleasure. His only fear was the possible drug charges against him and as far as the girls were concern there was no case. He was tried in court and found guilty on several charges and because he was allegedly here illegally they tried to get him deported back to Cuba. I don't know his final fate, but he was never seen again.

Case 4: Thou shalt not kill
I worked with different officers in the unit, but the most notorious was Rob. Rob was a tall slim Black cowboy. Now you must understand that this is Tucson

and you didn't see two Black officers working together, not in the 80's or early 90's. People would say how shocked they were to see two Black officers in the same vehicle. I think this was one of the reasons my Sergeant friend was always looked at through the evil eyes of the Administration because he dared to do things like this. This was unusual and when we would go to the park and check things out, we would come across Black transients who would be in awe at seeing us together. They would constantly marvel at the fact that there were two Black officers working together on the Force.

"Damn, ya'll must be detectives or something," they would say. "We didn't even know there were two Black officers in this whole city."

Rob took pride in being a Black cowboy and he could speak Spanish as well. Some of the "red necks" tried to denigrate him as a Black cowboy, but he believed in himself and that is what counted. I would tell him that all he had to do was believe in himself and understand that he didn't need anyone to validate him. He had a heart as big as Texas and he shared it with his family and he loved doing what cowboys do.

He was brought up in a Christian home and would slightly deviate once in a while from his true course, but God had his hand on him. I believe God has lassoed Rob and is waiting for him to stop jumping and tugging at the end of the rope so He can pull him in. I pray that when that moment comes he will just "let go and let God."

It appeared that when we worked together on cases, there was not one case that we couldn't solve. I think the case that hurt us the most emotionally was the one where one of the kids in the neighborhood had been involve in a homicide. After investigating this for several months and not being able to tie up loose ends, we learned that Nute (name changed) had turned his life around and had become one of the top athletes in the city. His eligibility had run out his senior year and the coaches and the school had allowed him to be a student coach. He was expecting perhaps a chance to go to college and play football.

When we had to arrest him it was painful. We found him at football practice and told him that we were bringing him in for questioning. Nute knew us and couldn't seem to stop telling us about his newfound life. He talked about the opportunities he had and his chances of going to college. He said he no longer was a part of the gangs in the neighborhood and our investigation had proven that to be true. He had broken contact with the hoods in the hood and was trying to keep his nose clean. The tragedy of this was his past sins had caught up with him. Fate had knocked on his door and only Nute could answer the knock.

The bible tells us that you reap what you sow. Nute had sowed and now it was his time to reap. He had committed the act, now he had to deal with the consequence. He was tried for murder and sent to Juvenile D.O.C.; Rob and I went to visit him on one occasion and he informed us that his girlfriend had a baby. I felt sad for him, because it seemed all his hope and help came too late. We must all remember, *"whatsoever a man sowest he shall reap" (Galatians 6:7,* **KJV).**

Case 5: Paco is loco!

We had a case involving a taxicab driver that had been beaten, shot at and left for dead. It apparently involved young men from the Indian Village. This occurred on or near the reservation site. Tucson had several sights around the city that belonged to the Native Americans and was considered part of the reservation. We worked closely with the Elders of the Tribes and they supported our investigation.

Rob and I were called out that night and the character of the suspects were similar to some of the Native American kids we knew that were always in trouble. It seemed that a couple of families lived next door to each other and they would fight constantly. It was rather ludicrous because even though they lived next door to each other, they would do drive-byes on each other's houses. When the two families were angry at each other, the boys at one location would do a drive-bye on their cousin's house next door. The next night the cousin would retaliate and shoot the cousin's house next door that had shot their house the night before. Fortunately, no one was ever injured.

We noted the description of the suspects and decided it was probably three or four of the Indian kids that were a part of this particular group. We didn't know exactly who they were, but we decided the next day we would take a chance and go talk to them. We decided among the two of us, which one of these young men would have the **most to lose.** Which one was **least involved** and who would be the **hardcore person** that wouldn't bulge. We found out that one of them had a girlfriend with a baby; another was a follower and the one that probably did it was Paco, because he was a hardcore gangster.

We had two things on our side; they didn't know that the taxi driver was alive and well, and they didn't know that Rob could speak Spanish. We made them all think the victim was in critical condition and not expected to live. They were looking at a possible murder rap.

The older of the three we will call Ruben. He was about to be married and his girl had a baby. He was at work when we visited his home. His girlfriend panicked and told us what he had said about his involvement in the incident. When he got home we advised him we had talked to the others and that they were trying to blame it on him. If he didn't do the shooting he'd better start talking. We also let him know that his girlfriend had already told us what he said about his involvement.

"Paco did it, man," he shouted. "Paco es loco" (Paco is crazy)!

Apparently they had visited an uncle that night and had stolen his rifle. They took a taxi from where they had stolen the rifle on the Southside to the reservation area on the Northside. Why a taxi cab driver would allow these individuals in his vehicle with a loaded rifle is beyond my understanding.

Ruben stated, "When we got to the reservation we didn't have any money so Paco decided we would rob the Cab Driver. When the car stopped we pulled him out of the car and threw him to the ground. We all either hit him or kicked him at least once." He was very nervous, but continued with his story, "Then while he was lying on the ground Paco aimed the rifle at him and shot. We didn't know he was going to do that."

You could tell that the telling of the story was like lifting a burden from his shoulder. He continued, "You could see the sparks on the road when he shot. The guy didn't move so we told Paco, let's get out of here and we ran." He took a deep breath and thought about Paco and his actions then said, "Damn man, he's crazy. Paco es loco! Sooner or later I knew he was going to kill somebody."

"Maybe he already has," we replied almost simultaneously.

Next we decided to talk to the one that was the weakest or the least involved before we talked to Paco. We knew it would be best to have the whole story by the time we came to Paco. He was the hardcore gangster and probably wouldn't talk. The weak suspect, we will call Lou. It was a pleasure just sitting and watching Lou squirm around in his chair in the interview room and we hadn't asked him any questions. He would ring out the sweat in his hands and come to the peephole to see if he could see anyone. We decided to let him squirm around for a while before we went in. We were at the station down town and had access to drinks, so we asked him if he wanted something to drink. He asked for a coke and that was ok, because anything with sugar in it would only make him more hyper and he was already nervous. We waited until the affects of the sugar had worn off somewhat and caught him at his low point.

We allowed him to assume that the victim was in the hospital and probably dying. We never said any of this, but we allowed him to believe it. That was all we needed, because he started delivering like a slot machine giving up the jackpot.

"Paco is loco," he said. "Damn fool probably killed that guy, huh?"

We taped the interview and he confirmed what Ruben had said, and now we had the scoop on Paco if he tried to deny anything. We could also make him fill in the blanks once he started talking and tried to leave out important information. It was now Paco's turn, and Rob and I carefully thought about our approach to interviewing him. He was nervous but tried hard not to show any emotions. We took another look through the peephole and observed his behavior before we decided to go in the room. We entered the room and we looked at each other and started shaking our heads.

"What do you think," said Rob, referring to Paco's situation?

"I don't know," I said, "probably first degree murder."

Paco began to sit up in his chair. He wondered if we were talking about him or another case.

"Well Homes," said Rob looking directly at Paco, "ain't much left for us to do but put the cuffs on and take your little ass to jail."

"I guess you're right," I said, "Ruben and Lou has already given us the story why are we dealing with him."

"Let's just throw his little ass in jail and go get something to eat," blurted Rob. "You know I have to eat something or my stomach hurts."

"I guess the right thing to do would be to interview him and see what he has to say, Rob," I said totally appearing to ignore Paco's presence.

Rob looked at his watch and said, "I think we got time, but let's get it over with. He'll probably lie about everything anyway."

"Should we tell him about the fate of the Cab driver," I whispered aloud?

"Nah, he'll start crying and carrying on," replied Rob. "I don't have time for that, man, I told you I need to go eat."

We started talking to ourselves and mentioning some of the details that we had gotten from the other two suspects. When Paco perceived that we had all the information we needed he couldn't wait to tell us his side of the story. His hardcore attitude was only a façade. When he realized he was standing out on a limb all by himself, and Rob and I had the saw in our hands he started to talk. We helped the situation by telling him that the cab driver was still alive and he would not be charged for murder. We didn't tell him that when he shot at the driver he missed completely and the cab driver was able to drive himself home that night after calling the police. He assumed that the driver was in the hospital fighting for his life in I.C.U. We simply allowed him to keep assuming. We later went to court and won the case. Paco was sent up for attempted homicide and the others did reasonable time and had to deal with the consequences of their actions.

Case 6: Kinfolk 1

I am the first to admit that the one thing an officer dread is having a run-in with a family member or kinfolk while in the performance of your duty. I must admit that I had this happen to me on more than one occasion. Once while in pursuit of a possible gang suspect my partner and I stopped a vehicle with possible suspects inside. My partner and I asked for a marked unit to pull the vehicle over for us. Once the officer had made the traffic stop, my partner and I approached the vehicle and commanded the occupants to exit the vehicle. They were very slow in obeying our commands so we withdrew our weapons and restated our command. The suspects exited their vehicle one at a time, but there was one subject that refused to cooperate and he had to be put to the ground and handcuffed. He appeared to be somewhat intoxicated and was belligerent as well. As I stood him up and leaned him against the car, I was surprised when he turned towards me and said, "Hi Unc (uncle) what's up?"

Another time I had stopped a suspected crack buyer in the South Park Area and was doing a field interview with the allege suspect. I saw paraphernalia in plan view and was waiting for my backup so I could further proceed with the investigation. Several officers arrived within a minute and secured the suspect as I proceeded to search the vehicle. We were in a residential area and the people were looking out of their doors hoping it wasn't one of their clients. Across the street was a house and while searching through the car I could hear the officers suspirations and making comments about a female that had walked out of the door of one of the houses. She was a very beautiful young lady and she had the attention of the officers. They were gazing at this young lady and mesmerized by her looks as she walked seductively across the street.

One of the officers got my attention and said, "Wow! Man you got to see this! There is one foxy lady coming towards us."

"See what," I replied as I stopped my search to see what the commotion was all about?

"Look at the dish that is coming in this direction," whispered an officer. "I wouldn't mind taking that home with me."

Another officer commented, "Hey, I think she wants to talk to you, she's coming your way."

I turned to face her as she approached and she was a very beautiful girl, but she looked familiar. She smiled at me and opened her arms to embrace me. Again I was surprised when she said, "Hi Uncle Lacey, how are you doing and how is Aunt Shirl" (referring to my wife)?

I then turned to look at the red faces of the officers who were embarrassed after finding out she was my Niece.

"Perverts," I said to them as they continued to stare at her butt as she walked away.

One of the saddest situations I had was with an individual I knew that worked for the Victim Witness Program. Early one morning I got a call from my other nieces and they said their mother, my sister had passed away in her sleep and they needed me to come over. My wife and I got there as fast as we could. When I arrived an Officer was there and I introduced myself as an officer and told him this was my sister and her family. He shared his condolences and continued his investigation nervously. I checked with him to see if he had done the necessary procedures involved in a D.O.A. call. He appeared to be new on the force and was receptive to my advice. He called Victim Witness to send someone by to talk with the family and I was looking forward to the assistance because the situation was painful and stressful for me. My sister was still in her bed and the children didn't want to leave her bedside. The emotions were very high and my wife was consoling them and trying to give them the moral and spiritual support they needed.

The officer responded when the Victim Witness person asked over the phone if anyone was there with him. He told them that I was there but the deceased was my family member. When V.W. personnel found out that I was there he asked to talk to me. You can't imagine how I felt when he said he had another call and asked if I could handle that situation. There I was left alone with the officer, OME and the children that had just lost their mother. I didn't want to be a Police Officer at that moment, I wanted to be a brother, an uncle and a person that had a right to grieve. It was even more disappointing when I had to help the mortuary attendant lift my deceased sister out of the bed, put her in a body bag and onto the gurney to take her to the medical vehicle. All the time the children were refusing to let go and crying vehemently for their mother. My perception of Victim Witness dropped below zero as I contended with the grief of the children that had lost their mother. I hope and pray that no other officer have to go through that with his or her family. Perhaps the Victim Witness Program can read this and change their policy that advocates this type of action.

Case 7: Kinfolk 2

It was a beautiful day in Tucson and it was hot as usual. I had been driving around the area on the Westside checking out the gangster hangouts when I heard a call asking officers to respond to the location near the front of the jail. The vehicle had been stopped on the street at this location. Officers had drawn their weapons on a subject they assumed was on PCP. He was a Black male involved in soliloquy (talking to oneself) and was sitting in a car in his underwear.

The vehicle was registered to a family I had known for years. The male was the father of two of my relatives (I won't say what the relationship is for the sake of the innocent). When I arrived officers had their weapons pointed towards the subject who was just sitting there in the vehicle partially nude. He was tripping on drugs and not responding to their commands. If he had made any wrong move even though his mind was totally oblivious of his surroundings and the fact that the officers were trying to communicate with him, I believe he may have been shot. When I arrived it was determined that he had not exhibited any weapons and was now standing outside of the car gazing at the officers and was very incoherent. It was apparent that his mind was not in the same world as we were.

I recognized the subject and my mind flashed back to what his girlfriend, who was my relative, had told me about him. They both had two children out of wedlock and he had been known to do PCP and other drugs in the past. She stated, on one occasion they were living in a three-story building and he was high on PCP (Superman Drug). He started taking his clothes off and telling her there were spiders crawling over his body. She helped him to get the clothes off thinking he may be telling the truth, but when he was nude there was no evidence of spiders. She then realized he was tripping off the drugs he had taken. Again he started screaming that spiders were on the walls and ceiling and he had to get away or they would eat him. He could feel them biting him all over his body and he was screaming and slapping himself as though he was knocking the spiders off of him. He ran towards the open window and jumped out. The apartment where they were living was located on the third floor. She screamed and ran to the window and to her surprise he was on his feet and running down the street naked. He was later subdued by friends and taken inside their home before the police could get to him.

She said she couldn't believe that he could jump out of a third floor window and not be hurt. Perhaps something may have broken his fall, but I told her the drug PCP has been known to give its users super strength.

I knew when I saw him that if I didn't do something he could be shot due to his bizarre behavior and the intensity of the situation. I went to the officer first on the scene and informed him that I knew the guy and I think I could talk him into coming with me. They had several violations on him and after giving them his name they discovered he had warrants. After receiving the ok from the officer in charge I approached the subject who was just standing by his vehicle talking to himself.

"Taye, Taye!" I shouted trying to get his attention. "It's me Lacey. Do you remember me?"

"Lacey is that you? Do you see him?" He was pointing towards the sun.

"See who Taye?" I knew it was someone in his mind and not someone real.

"Do you see God," he shouted?

"Where is God, Taye? Can you show him to me?" I said this trying to get his attention and to make him cognizant of my presence.

"He's all around us," he said as he twirled around in his underwear.

"Is there anyone else with God, Taye," I replied, again trying to get him to share with me his delusion.

"Do you see Tana and Shauna," I asked. These were his children and I was trying to get him now to think outside of his delusion.

"Tana and Shauna," he said, breaking away from his fantasy. "Where are they?"

"They are at home. Don't you want to go and see them?" Finally I had gotten through to him.

"Let me help you put your clothes on and we can go and see them. Would you do that for me?"

I spoke softly to him and tried to keep my voice at a level that would not excite him. He agreed and I helped him get dressed right there on the street. I told him that I had to put handcuffs on him before he could get in the police car and he conceded simply by not resisting as I put the cuffs on and lead him to the vehicle.

By this time the officers had put their guns away and were closer to us. Just in case he went off again they were in a better position to help subdue him.

I took him to the jail and while completing the necessary paper work he stood to his feet and started screaming, "Don't you see him...don't you see him!"

"See who Taye, God?"

"Yes," he shouted, "He's over there!"

He was looking at a block wall. With his hands cuffed behind his back, he ran towards the wall. It was as if he saw something beyond the wall and he ran into it head first trying to get to the other side. He never saw the wall, just the delusion. I dropped the paperwork I had and ran to him. His head was bleeding profusely and blood covered him. The wall was being sprayed with his blood as it squirted from his wound. He starred at the wall sprayed with blood, not feeling any pain and began commenting, "It's beautiful, it's beautiful. Isn't God beautiful," he said, as he appeared to calm down? The beauty of his own blood fascinated him as he continued his hallucination.

I was able to call an ambulance to come and transport him from the jail to Kino Hospital, because an ambulance had the necessary restraints. I followed the vehicle to the hospital and after arriving at Kino Hospital I thought I would call his home and advise a family member about his injury. I thought maybe one of his older brothers and sisters would come down, but instead his mother a missionary in the church, who was in her seventy's came.

It is so sad that many of the parents that are in church know nothing about what is going on in the world. They don't have a clue about drugs or the devastating effects drugs have on the mind and body. They are biblically knowledgeable, but not street wise.

When she arrived her son was still very delirious and incoherent. He didn't know who he was and continued returning to his trip via the PCP he had in his system.

"Taye, Taye, get up from here and let's go home!" she shouted.

"Mother," I said (because she was also a mother in the church), "he doesn't know who you are."

"Yes he does son," she said. "Taye, Taye what's wrong with you? Get up from here Taye and let's go home to the kids."

Her son was now mumbling words and talking to himself. She couldn't understand what was going on and by now I'm realizing this was a mistake.

She looked at me confused and helpless, "what's wrong with him? Does that stuff do that to him," she asked? "What is it that can take your mind like that?"

She was pleading for an answer that I knew would be difficult to explain to her.

"Mother, the drugs have him in his own little world," I replied. "He won't know who you are until he comes down from his high."

"He knows who I am son, he's just acting a fool," she replied totally ignorant of the effects of the drugs and the power it had over her son.

"No maam, he doesn't know who you are, but in time he will."

I felt sorry for her and ask that she go home and get some rest and I would stay with him until he came out of it. I advised her of the charges against him and that he would be transported to the jail when he got better. She sat patiently next to his bed rubbing his head and hoping that a mother's touch would bring him out of his predicament.

"Who are you, who are you," he said, as he looked at his mother? "Where is God? What did you do to God?"

I embraced her as she cried for him, "Lord help him, Lord help him," she said. We prayed for him and as we prayed he continued talking to himself. We

105

continued praying and she left saddened that her sick and injured son would later be taken to jail.

The bible tells us that, *"the effectual fervent prayers of a righteous man availeth much"* **(James 5:16, KJV).** I believe our prayer brought Taye through his ordeal.

The bible speaks against witchcraft (Galatians 5:20) and considers it as works of the flesh. Drugs are often listed under witchcraft because of the mind-altering effects they have on the brain. They induce a person to be delusional and create illusions within the mind. It is a tremendous source that Satan has to use against our children. We must "pray without ceasing" and *"trust in the LORD with all thine heart; and lean not unto thine own understanding. In all thy ways acknowledge him, and he shall direct thy paths"* **(Proverbs 3:5-6).** We must trust in God's word that, *"no weapon that is formed against thee shall prosper, and every tongue that shall rise against thee in judgment thou shalt condemn…"* **(Isaiah 54:17, KJV).**

Case 8: Mistake or not?

I had been in the gang unit for a while, and I was teamed without Rob who was African American. It seemed that our Sgt. Continued to defy the norm by allowing us to be together. I don't know what the problem was; perhaps the Department thought two Black officers together would insight a riot.

We were in plain clothes, but our guns and badges were visible, and it was obvious that we were officers. Rob had been on the force before me and had encouraged me to join years later. We saw a vehicle with a couple inside and they had left a notorious location. It was reported they were selling items out of their car. We waited until they left the area and called for a marked unit since we were in an unmarked vehicle. It was not procedure to stop vehicles in an unmark car. A motor unit heard our request and obliged us and stopped the vehicle. He was assisted by another vehicle. When I exited my vehicle we talked to one of the officers and thanked him for the stop, but the other officer was calling in information on his radio.

I approached the vehicle and there was a male sitting on the curb, and a female in the vehicle. I started to question her about selling clothes from the vehicle, and I was interrupted by a police command **"put your hands up and step away from the vehicle!"** I put my hands up and stepped away from the car, and I saw it was the motor officer that had responded to do the stop on the vehicle. He had his gun drawn and pointing at me and was giving me commands. I told him I would back away from the car, but he needed to look at my belt and he would see my gun and badge. Rob and the other officers saw this just in time and came running to where we were. They were yelling at the officer trying to tell him I was a police officer, but all he saw was a black man talking to a black woman. He too was shocked that Rob and I was riding together in the same car and was in the same unit.

There was no excuse for this, because I had been on the Department for at least five years. If it would have been night-time I may have been shot, because this fool didn't believe two Black officers could be in the same vehicle, or perhaps he thought most blacks were criminals.

Mistake or not, he never did apologize for what he did, and years later he was suspended temporarily when he and another black officer was feuding over some senseless pranks.

Case 9: Set up

I had returned to my office after patrolling the gang areas in the hood and was completing paperwork. I had to use the facilities so I took my radio with me. Afterwards I returned to my desk and continued my work. I realized my radio was missing, so I returned to the bathroom to retrieve it, but it was not there. I was puzzled because I swore I had taken it with me. I then decided I must have left it in my vehicle.

I received a phone call from someone stating they had found a radio, and they thought it was mine. I had forgotten where I last had it and when I asked the person where they had recovered it, they mention the area I had previously patrolled. The person on the phone stated they would hold the radio if I would come immediately and get it. I thanked them and was about to hang up the phone after getting an alleged location as to where the person would be, when the person on the phone asked me to do them a favor. I asked them what was their request and they stated they had received some citations and wanted me to fix their tickets. I told them that I didn't fix tickets and warned them about bribery. They then insisted that if I wanted the radio I would have to take care of their citations. I responded, "You can keep the radio and whatever punishment I received from the Department I will accept. I also let them know that to ask such a thing was bribery.

I heard laughing in the nearby office and I could also hear this over the phone. It was then I realized the person calling was in the office space next door. When I went to the office there were officers laughing along with the person that had called who was a Lieutenant. I retrieved my radio with a stern thank you and left the room. It was obvious that I didn't appreciate a Lieutenant trying to set me up.

They had found my radio in the bathroom, and thought it would be fun to try and set me up. I let the officers and the Lieutenant know that I disapproved of their deception and it was not comical. I learned that you have to be careful about whom you trusted, even with the men in blue.

Case 10: Dead in the church

I had known this young man since he was a child, and one day I saw him working on his car, while in the projects. Several of us had shown up and this person, I will call "Junebug" was involved in a conversation with the others about church.

"Ya'll all crazy," he belted, "there ain't no damn god. All the talk the preacher does is to get your money, so he can get bigger cars and fancy clothes."

"Boy, you better be careful what you say," retorted one of the fellows, "God don't like people using his name in vain."

"What the hell is he going to do, kill me? Well, here I am God take your best shot," he said as he stood mocking God in the open with his arms outstretched. He felt if God did not take his life; therefore, God does not exist.

"See," said another friend, "that's the kind of fool you don't want to be around when it's lightening; you might get struck down with him."

"I heard you are a policeman and you're preaching now," belted Junebug? "Well, I guess that's your problem."

"Why don't you go to church with me Junebug? Perhaps you will see things have changed," I said, hoping he would do it for me since he seemed to have some respect for me.

"I love you Codas, man," he responded, "but **you won't find me dead in the church."**

"Are you sure you won't go with me," I pleaded?

"Hell nah, like I said you won't catch me dead in the church," he shouted.

The following weekend, my friend came up missing. He was doing drugs and they found him lying on the grass dead from an overdose. It appeared he was trying to get to his apartment or a friend's apartment, but he didn't make it. There he lay dead on the grass, only a few feet from where he made his open challenge to God, to take his best shot."

A week later I went to Junebug's funeral, and as I sit there looking at his casket, I could hear his voice crying out, **"Hell nah, like I said you won't catch me dead in the church."**

The irony was he was dead and in the church. I was saddened by his departure, thinking that he never accepted Christ. But he could never say he didn't have the opportunity. I believe God had made him an offer that day, through my invitation to him to come to church and Junebug refused. It is written: **"be not deceived; God is not mocked, for whatsoever a man soweth that shall he also reap" (Galatians 6:7, KJV). I guess we did catch him dead in the church.**

Chapter VIII
School Resource Officer

I had been in the Gang Unit for almost five years and we did many drug raids and arrested gang bangers, but something was missing. I got tired of seeing dead kids after the fact. We were only moving the drug dealers and gangsters around the city from one place to another. Whenever the heat got turned up they left and went to another part of the city. We were not eradicating the problem we were simply transferring it from one place to another. I thought God has blessed me to teach and to counsel, perhaps by becoming a School Resource Officer I could make a difference. After being in Patrol, Gang Unit and Mirasol Task Force (twice) I decided to become an S.R.O.

I was sent to a Middle School that was approximately ninety-eight percent Hispanic. It appeared that the few other races of kids that attended soon left. With the bilingual education program in affect, most of the kids left there unable to speak English. I was blessed to learn a little Spanish and could speak just enough to get me in trouble. This school was totally into the Mexican culture and if it wasn't your culture you felt left out. If I felt that way, I'm sure those non-Mexican kids felt the same. I had the opportunity to talk to a couple of African American girls, but unfortunately they were on their way out. They stated there was no way that any other race beside Mexican kids, both National and American, could survive this school when everything in it and about it was leaning towards that culture. If there ever was segregation in disguised, this school was it. You had to be Mexican or be able to speak Spanish to be accepted there in the first place. The biggest conflict was between the two Mexican groups, those born here in the States and those from across the border (Mexico). Some were legal and others were not, but we paid for their education, health care and welfare.

I also had about five elementary schools I had to take care of, plus numerous projects that we had been volunteered to do. I taught the G.R.E.A.T. Program which was an acronym for Gang Resistance Education and Training. I found that since I had counseling skills and a Master's Degree in counseling that I had to do a lot of counseling as well.

I found out that School counseling is nothing like counseling people. It seemed that their counselors were more into teaching health and hygiene and advising the kids about what classes to take. They seemed to lack the skills to counsel kids one on one or deal with human conflict. Often I was asked to intervene between gang fights, family disputes and dissonance among the students. I had to mediate constantly between kids and kids, and kids and teachers and kids and their families. They had no concept of conflict resolution. I constantly dealt with drugs on campus, guns and what we called "mi' tote," which is the word for gossip or, "he said that she said and she said that he said," and it went on and on.

There were two women that were in charge and you could get exhausted just listening to them talk. I received an excellent view of Mexican culture and was baptized in the concept of female hysteria. They both could talk for a half an hour without taking a breath. They both talked to each other at the same time and could understand each other at the same time. Going into their office and listening to them talk to each other was like sticking your head into a beehive after it had been disturbed. With all their idiosyncrasies they did the best job they could in trying to keep peace and provide the school with a safe environment.

After being in that school for a while you had to check yourself and make sure you were in the United States. Most of the time you had to have an interpreter to speak to the students, their parents, and many of them were illegal.

I believe the School Counseling Programs should be revised into two different programs: The Counseling Program and The Advisory Programs:

1. **The Counseling Program:** should deal with one on one counseling, group counseling, family counseling, mediation, drug and alcohol counseling, drug education, conflict resolution and gang prevention/intervention education. It should assist those in the cognitive approach to some of their problems as well as Conflict Resolution and the concept of "Reality Therapy."

2. **The Advisory Program:** should deal with getting the kids into the right classes, getting them help if needed such as ADHD students, Language transition (for the Spanish speakers only students), Special Education students, Handicapped and Disabled students and directing all students to the proper resources within and without the School. This program should emphasize class placements and academic achievements.

I believe the most dangerous and influential period of a child's life is from Elementary through the Middle School years. If a child can survive middle school the whole household should celebrate and you should take them immediately to a specialist to be deprogrammed. They should also be debriefed so the information received can be used to help Middle School kids all over the world. Getting a child through Middle School is probably one of the greatest challenges a parent will have to face. When they have accomplished this they should sit down with other parents and disclose their secret.

When a child goes into Middle School, within months they become smarter than their parents and the rest of the world. We must find out what it is that causes them to think they have gained such a high degree of instant intellect and wisdom. Perhaps if we are able to isolate this factor, just maybe scientist can use it to rid all Middle Schools of their hormone problems and this perception of genius.

I would like to mention some of the cases or situations I was involved in while stationed at these various Middle and Elementary Schools. Perhaps after reading these cases you will agree with me that a change must come.

I must say I was not an Officer that dealt principally with the letter of the law, but also the spirit of the law. I just didn't want to know that you had committed a crime; I wanted to know why and what were the contributing factors. I tried to take everything in consideration before making an arrest. This is difficult when you are working under the auspices of "Zero Tolerance." The school didn't care about the person, the situation or circumstances, but that a crime was committed so, "arrest them!" It was their way of spanking the child, and I didn't like the idea of the kids getting extensive records for frivolous and childish antics.

I believe that in this day and time our children are not being punished immediately and that affects their behavior. If you did something wrong today, the law would punish them a couple of months later. I also realized that on many occasions the students had no sense of morals, ethics or values, which meant **(some) didn't know that what they did was wrong or against the law.**

What effect do you think being punished two months after the crime would have on their behavior before "that day" came? It has absolutely none. When these children go to court, half of them don't recall what they did to get there, and many had done the same things many more times, but didn't get caught. Many times they had to be reminded of what crime they had committed. The scripture tells us, *"Because sentence against an evil work is not executed speedily, therefore the heart of the sons of men is fully set in them to do evil"* (Ecclesiastes 8:11, KJV).

We are arresting our youth today for everything and anything. The charges are so severe that by the time many of them get to the age of eighteen they won't be able to get their drivers license, have their rights as a citizen or be able to go into certain professions, including our military and law enforcement or higher education.

Satan is trying to destroy the foundation of our children. He knows that if he merely knocks down their walls they can rebuild. So he destroys the foundation so they can't build. When they become eighteen there is nothing to build on. They have to start life without driver's license and having to work menial jobs because when they were nine and ten or fourteen and fifteen they got into trouble. One of the first questions on the application form is "have you ever been arrested?" The next one is "have you ever been arrested for a felony?" It continues with "have you ever committed a crime and have you ever been convicted of a crime." If you answer yes to any of the questions you don't have to go any farther.

The parents of a young man informed me about this situation: A child that accidentally touched his girlfriend's behind while walking with her. He walked her to the car and said goodbye (the boy was Black and the girl was White). A neighbor saw this and told the parent, who insisted that the thirteen year old who touched his girlfriend be arrested for child molestation. The parent brought the child to school the next day and **made** her press charges against the boy. The girl didn't remember her boyfriend touching her inappropriately, but was forced to concede to her mother's demand. The young lad went to court and admitted that he may have touch his girl's behind, but was not aware. He was convicted of a felony. It is evident that

111

by the time our children have grown out of their quandary stage, they have nothing to hold on to. Their hopes and their dreams have dissipated because of the things they did as a child.

I am reminded of the words of the Apostle Paul who said, ***"When I was a child, I spoke as a child, I understood as a child, I thought as a child; but when I became a man, I put away childish things"*** **(NKJ, 1Corinthians 13:11).**

What happens when that child becomes a man and there is nothing to build on for the future, because it has been taken away as a child?

The other problem with this age group is the people in authority over them haven't a clue about who they are. Most of our children and adults that are convicted and incarcerated are minorities. The people who are making life decisions for our children in the field of probation, parole and law enforcement are not minorities. They cannot relate to our children nor can the children relate to them.

The most common group of individuals that are in these areas is White middle class males and females. There is also a great influx of gay and lesbian personnel in all the areas of law enforcement. That includes: Police, Probation, Parole and Corrections. What that means is that we have these groups of individuals telling our sons and daughters how to be men and women, while on the other hand many of them have yet to decide who they are and what they are. How can you teach our young boys to be men, and girls to be women when you have an identity crisis yourself?

Don't get me wrong, because I have known many gay and lesbian officers that do a great job in their field. This isn't about their capability as an employee. I question the silent message they deliver to children that are already confused. No matter how hard you try, it is very difficult to teach and counsel an individual without allowing who you are and what you believe from interring into the class.

When a child tells you, "I want to be like Officer Gay because she doesn't need a man." That response isn't due to her ability to do her job, but it's about the message our children are receiving, whether verbal or non verbal. What message have she left behind and why? Elementary children are ignorant of the gay and lesbian life style, but middle school children can be influence and have the capacity to understand. They will try anything out of curiosity.

I believe that of all the assignments I had, being an SRO was both the most frustrating and the most rewarding. I think one of the biggest mistakes the schools have made is to include six graders in Middle School. Eight graders who are old enough to be in high school exploit them. The six graders have not developed both mentally or physically enough to deal with the depth and extreme of Middle School corruption. There are sixteen year olds in Middle School with kids that are eleven and twelve years old.

I would like to present to you the following cases, which make up only a few of the hundreds of cases that were reported.

Case I: Middle School Witch

I was in my office at the Middle School when a six grader was brought in to my office for theft. She had taken money from one of the after school's programs. She also had marijuana in her possession. I questioned her about both issues and she stated she had no choice. She believed that her friend was a witch and if she didn't do what she wanted, a spell would be placed on her.

"A witch," I replied?

"Yes, Mister, Melissa is a witch," she said with a Mexican accent.

"Why would you say she is a witch," I replied inquisitively?"

"The other day when she was with her grandparents she asked them for some money and they refused," said the student. "She stole the money instead and when they found out they punished her. She got angry and took some of her grandfather's hair, clothing and a few other things and she put a curse on him," she nervously stated.

"What kind of curse," I inquired?

"Didn't you hear Mister, her grandfather had a heart attack and might die," she belted, surprised that I didn't know the details about her friend, the alleged witch.

"Why should I know that, when there are hundreds of kids going to this school," I replied? "I don't know who you're talking about."

"The whole school is talking about it," she boasted. "She told them (other students) about the spell and a few days later her grandfather is in the hospital because his heart no work."

"What has this to do with you taking money and bringing drugs to school," I asked?

"Mister, she told me if I didn't take the money and give it to her, she would put a curse on me," she replied. "This morning on the way to school she had some marijuana and said if I didn't hold it for her, she would put a curse on me."

At this point she started trembling and broke into tears. It was evident that she was terrified of Melissa, the alleged witch.

"She made animals disappear," she said as she sat sobbing. "She made my cat disappear and it never came back. If I didn't do what she said I would be cursed with a sickness and die!" She continued crying as I took a Kleenex from the box and handed it to her. She seemed to be lifting a burden by telling me about her friend the witch. One thing I have learned is "perception is a reality" with children.

I calmed her down and then asked for Melissa to be brought to my office. I promised her I wouldn't allow Melissa to hurt her. I had her to wait in another room while I talked to Melissa.

Melissa was little over weight and appeared to be just as nervous as her friend.

"So you're the witch," I blurted out?

She put her head down, afraid to look at me as I spoke to her. Then she began making sounds that was not natural for a child.

"Look at me when I'm talking to you," I said. "You claim to be a witch but "whatever spirit that guides you, I rebuke that spirit in the name of Jesus Christ do you hear me?"

She spoke in a deep rough voice and said, "YEESS I HEARR." It was not her voice.

I knew it was the spirit within her that had spoken. So I put one hand on my bible and spoke with the authority, "In the name of Jesus Christ I command you to go!"

She started to shake and then her body relaxed. Whatever was there decided to leave for the moment.

"Melissa, Melissa," I said, as I slightly tapped my desk with a pencil. Her eyes were closed and she appeared to be in a trance. I banged the end of my desk with my bible that had replaced my pencil and her eyes opened. She started to cry like the child she was and my heart went out to her.

"I sorry, I sorry," she cried in broken English.

"What are you sorry for Melissa?"

"I sorry for hurting my 'Tata' (grandfather), I sorry for getting me friend in trouble and I sorry for being a witch," said Melissa apologizing for her actions.

I came from behind my desk and handed her my bible.

"Hold this please," I requested. "Do you go to church?"

"Yesss," she responded in a normal voice.

"Do you believe in God?"

"Yesss I think so," she said again still in a normal voice.

I thought about the scripture that says, *"No servant can serve two masters; for either he will hate the one and love the other, or else he will be loyal to the one and despise the other. You cannot serve God and mammon"* (Luke 16:13, KJV).

"Honey you can't believe in God and go around trying to be a witch," I said. "You can't serve God and the Devil at the same time."

By now she was starting to look and acted like a normal child. After handing her my bible, I said, "Hold this close to you as we talk." She did and she appeared more and more relax as we talked.

I asked what had happened to the money, and she said she had given it away to students so they would like her. I prayed with her in the office and she was relieved to know that she didn't have to be a witch to get friends. She named most the students she had given the money to and within hours most of it was recovered. She claimed she had stolen the marijuana from an older sister's room.

The word got around by word of mouth, and most of the students that brought the money back were very nice and said they figured she had stolen it, and they were afraid to spend it. There was a few that gave it no thought. They all did something extra nice, when they told her she didn't have to give them money to be her friend. The reason she wanted to be known as a witch was to get friends, but it was that very concept that had turned them away.

I also noticed she had cut-marks up and down her arm. She said she did it to punish herself when she did wrong. She was becoming a cutter (a person who self mutilate). I had been in the gang unit for years and these were obvious signs of Satanism, the torturing and killing of animals, and the alleged spells. I thought it best to talk to her parents or guardian.

I decided to release her to her grandparents, but was told that the grandfather was ill and the grandmother was blind. The child's uncle came and I released her to him after giving him the information that was given to me. Surprisingly, he was a Priest and was dressed in his clergy attire. When I told him about her wanting to be a witch he brushed it off as nothing. I also advised him that the marijuana came from the older sister who lived in the house. Again he brushed it away and said she probably found it on the way to school. I confronted him about these things and why would she blame a sister when all she had to say in the beginning was, I found it? When I brought her in she told him the same thing, but again he denied it to be the truth. He did say they had found dead cats around the house lately and birds without heads and that she had cut herself with different objects, but it was probably an accident.

"The headless birds were an accident as well," I asked? "I guess they were just flying around when their heads fell off," I retorted, "and the cats probably saw these headless birds and died of a heart attack, or committed suicide?"

I don't think he ever got the sarcasm because it went right over his head. "The mutilation of animals is also a sign of the occult worship or Satanism," I explained. I also told him that you could trace the childhood of many with anti-social behavior and you would find a record of self-mutilation and animal mutilation. He totally ignored my attempts to educate him, and he signed the release and took her away. I never saw her again. I guess he was a priest that didn't believe in the supernatural.

Case 2: Prostitute at Twelve

A young girl was brought to my office because she did not fit the dress code and she had a great deal of money in her possession. The principal called the parents and they said they didn't have any money missing. I talked with the student about the enormous amount of money and she claimed she got the money from men.

"Doing what," I replied.

"Making them feel good," she stated, "Whatever it takes to make them feel good."

"How old are you," was my next response?

"Thirteen," she said.

"How long have you been making men feel good to get their money," I enquired?

"A year," she said, "my parents know, but they never say anything."

"Do you have a boyfriend," I asked?

"Yes but not here at the school; my boyfriend is twenty-two years old, and he picks me up at home. My parents have met him and they think he is a nice guy."

I was surprised, but I was not shocked because while patrolling after school I would see cars with many older boys there picking up the Middle School girls. Several times there were cars with University of Arizona stickers on the car and the boys were not their brothers. If they were, then we also had an incest problem, because they would be pretty intimate while picking them up from school.

When the parents came, I told them about the source of the money their daughter had acquired. They said it wasn't their business. They also claimed they had given the boyfriend the ok to date their thirteen year old daughter and had the audacity to say, "We don't think he minds that she is thirteen."

It was apparent they were benefiting from this relationship and he wasn't her boyfriend, but her pimp. I notified Child Protective Services, but never received any feedback on this situation. They took the daughter home with them and all the money. I didn't see her again.

Case 3: Personal Property

There were probably more drugs, gangs and fights at this Middle School than any other school in the city. I was amazed how Satan worked in this school. The children begin to point out differences among themselves even though they all were predominately Mexican.

They made a difference between the Mexican students born in the U.S.A. and those born in Mexico, between the dark skin students and light skin Mexicans, between the way they dressed, and if they could or could not speak English. They made a difference between their economic statuses.

They loved jewelry and it was the origin of many fights. Someone would take by force, steal or borrow jewelry and not return it. Girls would wear their mother's wedding rings to school to show them off. How can your mother not know her wedding ring is missing?

Their sense of morals, value and integrity was lacking, because they switched sides every day. You had group fights (non-gang) and gang fights involving certain girls and the next day you would have another fight with a couple of the girls switching their alliance. It was no big deal to borrow someone's clothing or jewelry and then loan it to someone else.

The boys had a very macho attitude and the young girls felt they were their property. I remember talking to a girl whose ex-boyfriend slapped her around. When she came to the office she had bruises on her face and was angry.

"What happen and who did it," was my first words?

"It was my x-boyfriend Ramon. Hell, he don't have the right to be slapping me around or beaten on me," she shouted. "I ain't his bitch no more!"

"So if you were still his girl he would have the right to beat on you and slap you around," I retorted?

"Hell yeah, don't you know that's just the way it is," she belted with pride. "But he ain't my man no more, so he shouldn't be f---king touching me."

I took the first few minutes telling her that you don't disrespect me or my office by using profanity. "Constant profanity is a sign of a limited vocabulary," I stated. I don't know if she understood me or not but she settled down. I took an hour trying to explain to her that Ramon had no right to hit her even if she was his girl. She was a person and not his property.

I was adamant when I said, "being someone's girl does not give them the right to beat on you and you need to respect yourself and realize you are not anyone's bitch. A bitch is a female dog and you're not a dog."

She was serious when she said, "you mean that asshole didn't have the right to hit me when I was his girl?"

"NO! He didn't," I replied.

"Damn," she said, "that's the way it is at home too!"

Again I shouted, "Hey watch the language young lady!"

She didn't want to press charges against Ramon, so I let her go after bringing Ramon in to apologize. He figured if he apologized he wouldn't be arrested.

Later I had to teach a class on drugs and its consequence. I went to the class and it had Special Ed kids involved. I talked to them about drugs and its affects on the human body and on students that are between the ages of puberty. I told them what the affects of cocaine, heroin and marijuana had on the body.

They were surprised when I told them that marijuana smoking could affect your sexual development at this particular age. The ovaries could be affected and though you may later decide to have children you could have a deformed child. When I told them that little girls and boys hormones are affected and boys have been known to have undeveloped genitals and grow breast and girls have been known to grow hair on their chest, it seemed to get their attention.

I was touched when a student walked into my office after the class and put his pipe and drugs on my desk. He was trying hard to hold back the tears but he lost the battle.

"I no want to do this, no more," he said in broken English.

"I hear you in class and this drug is bad for me, *Estes no Buenos* (this is no good)!" He said. "You put me in jail, its ok, *perro no mas* (but no more)."

I wondered when I left the class if I had gotten through to anyone. God showed me that someone was listening. I took the drugs into evidence and talked to his parents, but did a referral. I believe in my heart if I touched only one, then I was successful.

Case 4: OSA (Bear)

She was a Native American girl from the reservation, stocky with dark brown eyes and black hair. She was dress like a boy but she wasn't trying to be a tomboy. She was trying to be tough. She was sporting gang attire and colors and had been brought into my office for fighting. Her nickname was Osa. Osa or Oso means "Bear" in Spanish, and it was the name the students had given to her.

God had allowed me to see her through his eyes and though many saw her as an ugly caterpillar, I saw beyond the metamorphosis and beheld a beautiful butterfly. She was given that name not because she had the courage of a bear or the spirit of the bear but because of her rugged appearance. She tried everything within her power to be that explicit image the students had painted even down to her walk. She would sway from side to side as she walked shifting her balance from one foot to the other. Her hair was not combed, her clothes were a couple extra sizes too big, but I could tell she was clean.

She sat before me as a solid block of ice, but as I begin to tell her of the beautiful person I saw in her and the potential she had to be whatever she desired in life, the ice begin to slowly melt. I told her that at that moment she had presented herself as "a nobody," but it was up to her to be "somebody." I told her I was also a pastor of a church and ask if I could pray for her that she would have the strength and desire to be herself. She said her relatives were Christians and as I prayed she melted down to pure water and the warmth of her tears contributed to the warmth that now resided in her heart.

I invited her relatives in the office and we talked and I told them everything I had done. I wasn't surprised when they said they went to church and would be praying for her.

"She thinks she's ugly," said her aunt, "but she is a very beautiful Indian girl."

"She thinks because they call her Osa she has to act tough like the bear," said another, "but all she needs is the courage and the spirit of the bear."

"Yes maam," I replied, "and the bible tells us, *"the Lord takes pleasure in His people; He will beautify the humble (meek) with salvation"* (Psalms 149:4, KJV).

When they left I could see that Osa had listened and pondered in her heart what was said that day. I never her saw again until about six months. She came into the office with the principal.

The principal said, "Do you know who this is?"

I didn't recognize her because she had changed from the rough and grumpy look.

"I'm sorry, but I don't quite recognize her," I said embarrassed.

She told her to turn around so I could take a look at the way she was dressed, but I still could not place her. This person had her hair combed and looked like a young lady.

"It's Osa," she said! Don't you remember?"

"Yes, I do, but what happened to you," I questioned as I starred at her for a response.

"She is our student of the month and have been awarded the most improved student in the school," said the principal.

I got out of my chair to shake her hand, but instead she embraced me. I felt such a joy for her and yet I was still in disbelief over her astounding change. When the principal left the room we talked.

"I went to church and gave my life to Christ," she said, "and the Lord has turned me around."

That year I rewarded her by taking her with me to a picnic sponsored by the Police Department to honor certain good students. Those who had made certain achievements were given gifts, accolades and a picnic in their behalf.

I am reminded of the story of David when Samuel went to the house of Jesse in search of a king. The Lord said to Samuel, ***"Do not look at his appearance or at the height of his stature, because I have refused him. For the Lord does not see as man sees; for man looks at the outward appearance, but the Lord looks at the heart,"*** (1Samuel 16:7, KJV).

I was there at the school long enough to see her graduate and I believe she will succeed in all her endeavors, because she not only have the spirit and the strength of the bear, but most important the Spirit of God.

Chapter IX: Conclusion
Running a spiritual race on and earthly track

We must all understand that any of these cases could have been us. I can truly say, but by the grace of God there goes me. We are all in a spiritual race. There is a spirit behind the character of man. When we see negative/positive behavior in people we must understand there is a spirit (s) that instigates and influences us to act.

This race that we run is a spiritual race and we are not running against other Christians, the adversary is spiritual. **Ephesians 6:12 tells us:** *"For we wrestle not against flesh and blood (people), but against principalities (master spirits), against powers (powers of evil and satanic beings), against the rulers of the darkness of this world (princes of darkness), against spiritual wickedness (wicked spirits) in high places (not just this world but the spiritual world)."* **1Peter 5:8** continues by telling us to, *"be sober, be vigilant; because your adversary the devil, as a roaring lion, walketh about; seeking whom he may devour."*

You must be sure to register before you start running. **Romans 10:9** tell us how to register: *"...if thou shalt confess with thy mouth the Lord Jesus, and shalt believe in thine heart that God hath raised him from the dead, thou shalt be saved. For with the heart man believeth unto righteousness; and with the mouth confession is made unto salvation."* If you do that and you will be registered.

Though we are running a spiritual race on an earthly track we need power (energy). **Acts 1:8 says, "...**Ye shall receive power, after that the Holy Ghost is come upon you" (KJV).** It is the Spirit that enables us: *"not by might, nor by power, but by my spirit, saith the Lord of hosts."*

When we prepare to run this race we do not dress for speed, because this race is more like an obstacle course where at times you may have to fight. So instead of light track shoes, a pair of shorts and a T-shirt: put on the whole armor of God as stated, *"...Having your loins girt about with truth, the breastplate of righteousness, your feet shod with the preparation of the gospel of peace; the shield of faith; the helmet of salvation, and the sword of the Spirit, which is the word of God"* (Ephesians 6:13-17, KJV).

Hebrews 12:1 states, *"...let us lay aside every weight, and the sin, which doth so easily beset (trouble, harass, attack) us, and let us run with patience the race that is set before us, Looking unto Jesus the author and finisher of our faith..."*

Running a spiritual race is hard enough but when you are hindered by an earthly track it is impossible to finish without God. When you're running obstacles keep popping up on the track. You may have to run through bad relationships, financial problems, bad leadership; troubles on the job, lies, back biting, sickness and sorrows but keep running.

Most tracks are protected from strong winds. But the race of life is run in both good and bad weather: Just like Paul told Timothy, *"Preach the word; be instant in season, out of season"* **(2Tim 4:2, KJV)**. You must run both in season and out of season, when you feel like running and when you don't feel like running.

When you are running don't look back. Jesus said, **(Luke 9:62, KJV)**, *"No man, having put his hand to the plough, and looking back, is fit for the kingdom of God."* So whatsoever you do don't look back.

The race is not to the swift, nor the battle to the strong…. but he that endures to the end shall be saved. Remember to trust in the Lord at all times and keep your eyes on the prize and don't stop prematurely. Paul said, *"…I count not myself to have apprehended: but this one thing I do, forgetting those things, which are behind, and reaching forth unto those things, which are before. I press toward the mark for the prize of the high calling of God in Christ Jesus"* **(Philippians 3:13, KJV)**.

I say to all the Cops for Christ, when you start to get discouraged keep on running. You may start feeling the affects of age and arthritis, and rheumatism may try to hinder you, but keep on running. Your eyes may get dimmer, your steps may get shorter and your body may start leaning from the wear and tear, but keep running. You can be lame, deaf and blind, and you can still run this race. You don't need hands or feet, eyes or ears, education or money to run this race. Don't use your sickness or affliction as an excuse to try and get out of the race: *"present your bodies a living sacrifice; holy, acceptable unto God, which is your reasonable service"* **(Rom. 12:1, KJV)**.

When you start to get close to the end you may feel a bit discouraged, but keep running. You can get rest on the other side. **Job said, *"… In death the wicked cease from troubling, and there the weary are at rest"* (Job: 3:17, KJV). David said, *"Oh, that I had wings like a dove! For then I would fly away and be at rest"* (Ps. 55:6, KJV).**

Don't worry about having a place to go when the race is over. Jesus said to his disciples, *"Let not your heart be troubled: ye believe in God, believe also in me. In my Father's house are many mansions: if it were not so, I would have told you. I go to prepare a place for you. And if I go and prepare a place for you, I will come again, and receive you unto myself; that where I am, there ye may be also and whither I go ye know, and the way ye know"* **(John 14:1-4, KJV)**.

I don't know how far you come in this race but Christ said to the church at Thyatira, *"that which ye have already hold fast till I come. And he that overcome, and keepeth my works unto the end, to him will I give power over the nations…and I will give him the morning star"* **(Rev: 2:25-26, 28, KJV)**.

I am speaking to Law Enforcement Officers and others. We must run with patience, run righteous and run holy. Keep your eyes on Christ and keep running until you hear a voice say *"well done."* I'm running for the well-done, eternal life, a crown of righteousness and the crown of glory that fade not away.

Jesus Christ is God, and **He is so powerful** that he spoke to a storm and the wind and waves ceased; **He is so humbled** that he got on his knees and washed the dirty feet of his friends; **He is so passionate** that when he saw the suffering of Mary and Martha after their brother Lazarus died, and when he saw the future destruction of the City of Jerusalem and he wept; **He is so approachable** that little children came running into his arms.

Perhaps one day when we face our maker, hopefully I am found in the section that says, "Cops for Christ." When the Lord calls my name I shall be glad to say, "Here am I," and hopefully He will say to me WELL DONE!

I would like to thank all the police officers that have shared with me a portion of their life as we walked "the beat" on the road of life. To those who have lost loved ones in this field, I say to you may God give you the strength to carry on. I would like to conclude with the Benediction of the Apostle Paul to the saints at Corinth: ***"Finally, brethren, farewell. Become complete, be of good comfort, be of one mind, live in peace; and the God of love and peace will be with you"*** **(2 Corinthians 13:11, KJV).**

The end

Made in the USA
Charleston, SC
29 October 2010